Kiss Every
STEP

A Survivor's Memoir from the Nazi Holocaust

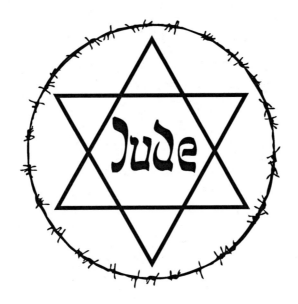

Doris Martin
with Ralph S. Martin

Doris Martin

DEDICATION

This story is dedicated to our mother, Perla Baila Szpringer, who died only a few months after World War II ended. Before the end of the war, Mother said that she had only one dream to fulfill, which was to see all her children once more, safe and healthy after the war. After that, she did not care what happened to her. Miraculously, her dream was realized. It is also dedicated to those six million who were so cruelly murdered, and cannot tell their own stories.

ACKNOWLEDGMENTS

We would like to thank all of those friends who have helped with this project:

Foremost, my brothers Moishe and Issa Springer, whose losses we feel deeply, and my wonderful sister, Rae Harvey. Their testimonies have been the basis for most of this book, often at great emotional stress for them to return to painful memories.

We want to thank Sandra Lubarsky, Stephen Stern and Fred Kronen for their suggestions, and practical and moral support; Greg Larkin for his extensive work in getting this book started; Lyle Graham for his writing tips; our niece, Jerri Martin, for her editing, critique and suggestions; and our friend Maxine Rusche for her diligent job of proof reading.

For assistance in publication we wish to thank Ben Gurion University of the Negev, especially President Rivka Carmi, Amos Drory, Daniel Sivan, and our good friend Philip Gomperts.

Doris and Ralph Martin

PREFACE

This story has been committed to paper for me and my family by my husband Ralph, after extensive interviews and travels with me, my sister and my brothers. Unfortunately my brother Josef, for whom these events are still too painful to relive by discussing them, has participated minimally in this process. In this story, I'm referred to as "Dora", as that was my name in Poland, and we have used the family's name of "Szpringer", as it was in Poland. We changed the family name to "Springer" when we came to America.

The story is narrated in first person by me and by my siblings, when they were more closely involved in the events and where I was largely absent. Each episode has been related as it was told by those persons involved.

A short note on spelling of Polish names and places: Polish spellings have been used as much as is practical. A few letters in the Polish alphabet are not in the English alphabet. Such letters have been transliterated to the approximate English equivalents, with the exception of the Polish letter "Ł" or "ł", which is pronounced closely to the English "w".

Wherever possible, the actual names of persons in the story have been used; however, the real names of a few persons have been forgotten, and therefore, invented names have been assigned to them.

FOREWARD

The story I'm about to tell is the true story of my family, the Szpringer family of Bendzin, Poland. We were just one among millions of ordinary Jewish families caught up in the Nazi Holocaust. My parents had five children, and what is exceptional about my family's story is that all seven of us survived the Holocaust. Each of us has a unique story to tell. My oldest brother escaped from Poland to Russia and was sent to a slave labor camp by the Russians; I lived through the concentration camps; the rest evaded capture in a number of remarkable ways.

I know of no other large Jewish family in Poland who survived the Nazi slaughter. Most families had no survivors. Some more fortunate families had one or two survivors. For an entire Polish Jewish family of seven people to have survived the Holocaust is truly amazing, and perhaps unique. I would like to point out that there was nothing special about our family that would have marked us for survival. That is, we were not especially smarter or more determined than those who were murdered. The vast majority of the victims were not in a position where any action on their part could have saved them. Our family was extremely fortunate to be in a position where we could use our survival instincts to make a great many life saving decisions, many in a split second, which coupled with tremendous luck and perhaps some miracles, allowed us to survive, and to bear witness. Neither I, nor any of my family, know why we were chosen to live when others died; we were certainly no more deserving of life than those who perished, but we hope that by telling our story we will help to assure that those millions of poor souls who suffered and died so horribly will not be forgotten, but will be remembered for what they were—not statistics, but real people who had a love of life and the right to live. This is our story:

SZPRINGER FAMILY	FORGED POLISH NAMES
Father- Abraham	Jan Drzewo
Mother- Perla Baila Golenzer	Bronslowa Fletzau
Son- Isaak (Issa)	
Son- Moishe	Mieczyslaw (Mietek) Scrowronski
Son- Josef (Yossel)	Jusek Fletzau
Daughter- Dora	
Daughter- Laya	Poilka Flatzau

CHAPTER ONE

The Innocent Life

"Stop, Stop! Go back! I'm sure that was it."

My companions don't know why I'm so excited, but obligingly turn the car around at the first opportunity.

"Stop! Pull over here. Yes, I'm sure that's it. That *is* the house. See those steps in front—and over there on the left, there's the garden. And look! Across the street—see the tall smoke stack. That's the factory that belonged to the Nazi who owned the house. Too bad Moishe didn't come with us. I know he'd recognize it, for sure. This is amazing! This is really a miracle! We were just driving by and out of the corner of my eye, I see this house. This is where we all came together after the War– all seven of us, even Issa, who came back all the way from Siberia. Oh, I wish Rae could be here. She won't believe that I found it, after what—almost 60 years? Isn't it something? If we hadn't just happened to come down this street to buy gas we'd never have found it."

This house is in Nowa Ruda, Poland, just a few short miles from the remnants of the Ludwigsdorf Concentration Camp, where I spent nearly three years as the unwilling guest of Hitler and his murdering henchmen. But this is a long story, so I'd better start at the beginning:

In 1915, a young Jewish couple, Abraham Szpringer and his new wife Baila, my parents, were married and started their family in Bendzin, Poland, approximately 20 miles north of Oswiencim, the ordinary little Polish town not yet known to all the world as Auschwitz.

My father was born in the small shtetl of Zharki (with about 3500 Jews), about 20 miles, as the crow flies, northeast of Bendzin. His father, Chameljoel, eked out a living as a hard-working shoemaker. It seemed that in those days, just about every other Jewish man was either a shoemaker or a tailor, and all of them were barely making ends meet. I never knew my grandmother Gitel, as she died before I was born. Grandfather remarried (at the age of 93), and died at the age of 102. Fortunately, he died shortly before the Nazis devoured Poland, so he was spared the horror that followed.

The exact year of my father's birth has always been a matter of some debate, but was somewhere around 1886. Following the custom of the time, my father spent his boyhood and teen years learning his father's trade, but, before he could go into business for himself he was hauled off into the Russian army as soon as he became of draft age, since this part of Poland was under Russian control. Although he never looked back upon his time in military service with much fondness, he often spoke with pride of the time that he paraded before the Czar. Several years after this stint in the army, he was again drafted. By this time he had married and had absolutely no interest in soldiering, so he took "French leave", and went back home. Probably because there were so many men who fled the army, and with communication not being then what is today, he simply kept a low profile, and was never caught.

Baila Golenzer's family was slightly better off, having a small, but thriving business selling shoes in Bendzin. But Mother's family suffered a tragic loss when she was only a young teen. Her mother died giving birth to her seventh child, and my grandfather died not long afterward. Mother, little more than a child herself, but being the eldest child, took on the unenviable task of raising six young siblings, one being a mere infant. Her relatives realized that this unfortunate situation could best be resolved by finding a husband for young Baila. This was easier said than done, for although she was an attractive young girl, not every young man would want to start out in life by taking on the "baggage" she would bring with her? Into this picture stepped young Abraham. Here was a poor, but healthy, young man, properly religious, but with very few career prospects, in a country where making a living was anything but easy.

Their marriage was primarily one of convenience, not the result of romance, but both were content with the arrangement. Sympathetic relatives took in the other five orphaned children, while Mother and Father raised the baby, Shloimo, as their own. In accordance with traditional Jewish custom, at her marriage, Mother shaved her head and wore a wig and scarf for the rest of her days.

Mother gave birth to eight children of her own, but sadly, three of them died in infancy. The death of each baby brought sorrow that only a mother can understand, but losing three of eight children was not unusual in those days when good medical and proper prenatal care were a distant dream. Of the surviving children, my brother Isaac (called Issa) arrived first, born in 1916, followed by Moishe in 1918, Josef (called Yossel) in 1922, me in 1926, and then in 1929 they gave *me* a wonderful present, my little sister Laya, who is still my dearest friend. Uncle Shloimo was another member of the family, and I always thought of him as an older brother.

Only patches of grass cover the bumpy ground where our house once stood, where I spent my early carefree childhood. Even the charred ruins have been cleared away. But I can still picture this home, where I drew my first breath of life, as did my sister and my brothers. Our home was a small apartment on the ground floor of a large three story building, shared by maybe twenty other Jewish families living in their own small apartments. Only a few rich families in Bendzin could afford their own houses.

Our apartment was both our home and our place of business. The building fronted on the Alte Marek—the old market—which made it a great location to do business. During the weekdays Father supported his family by selling shoes, which were stored in the back room. It was a common practice for people to have their businesses in their homes in those days. He sold mostly higher quality shoes which he bought mostly from his special connections in Germany. The secret to beating his competition was to buy right. He followed the principle, "If you buy right the selling will take care of itself".

Our lifestyle was quite simple. We had no carpet, no refrigeration, not even an icebox, and no running water. Our toilet was a row of privies outside, which were shared by the entire apartment building. In place of a carpet, Mother spread burlap potato sacks on the floor for warmth and to keep dirt off the wooden floor. When the sacks got dirty, we took them outside and gave them a good shaking. In spite of the sacks, Mother spent many hours on her hands and knees scrubbing the floor with a brush, soap, and water. For her, cleanliness was, indeed, next to godliness.

Since we lived in a coal mining district, coal was cheap, so we used it for both heating and cooking. Every day Mother had to start the fire in the big cast iron cook stove with some kindling and paper, and wait until the coal was burning well before starting her cooking. The rest of our home was kept warm by a ceramic tiled heating stove. In the winter one kid or another would quite often be sent out for more coal to keep the fire hot, and a well-beaten path was trod in the snow between the back door and our coal shed outside next to the building. In those days, the idea that somebody would steal coal never entered our minds, so everyone's coal sheds were left unlocked all the time.

Our coal shed was never empty, thanks to the reliable coal-seller, who drove through the snow from house to house with his horse and wagon, and lugged heavy gunny sacks full of coal to each coal shed. In spite of having all the work he could handle in the winter, the coal-seller was rewarded with very modest payment for his hard, dirty labor, and was among the poorest of the town's citizens.

With all the factories also burning coal, it's small wonder that throughout Poland the air we breathed was full of soot and sulphur fumes, and the buildings were almost black. Undoubtedly, those who lived far from the cities were blessed with a longer lifespan.

We had no water in our apartment building. There was a pump outside in the market place, from which every family had to draw its water and carry it home in buckets. We emptied the buckets into a large wooden tub on a table in the kitchen. Come washing day this meant a lot of trips to the pump, but we were lucky to live on the first floor; those living on the third floor got a lot more exercise. Every week Mother scrubbed the family's clothes on a wash board, using a scrub brush on the tough stains, thoroughly rinsed them, and then hung them on the line outside to dry, except in winter or rainy weather, when she had to haul them up to the attic to hang them. as soon as we were old enough, Laya and I were recruited to help her with this chore. Mother scrupulously ironed everything by heating the heavy cast-iron iron on the cook stove. This was a very hot job in the summer, so she tried to start as early in the morning as possible.

As a child, before the war, I never saw an automobile, anywhere. Horses, streetcars, and trains were our only means of getting around, other than walking, which we did a lot of; which helps to explain why shoemaking was such a common trade. There were some bicycles, but I never rode one; in fact I never saw a girl or woman riding one. I'm sure it was not considered proper. We had no air pollution from internal combustion engines, but by the process of internal digestion the horses created another form of pollution, and with as many horses as went up and down the street, the odor could be pretty potent. When the winter snow piled up there was a shift from horse-drawn wheeled vehicles to horse-drawn sleighs and sledges. Since the roads were never cleared, but just constantly packed, any thawing revealed an especially nasty mess.

Looking back, our life may have seemed hard, but we didn't think of it that way, it was just the way it was, and better than our grandparents who didn't even have electricity. Since we didn't have television to isolate us from each other, we were never lonely.

The best thing in those carefree years as a little girl was playing with my best friend Rutka. We loved to skip rope, toss balls, and play hop-scotch, and of course, we did a lot of giggling together. Rutka and I had more in common than just the love of playing. We were born on the exact same day: December 25, 1926. Sometimes we would just wander around the neighborhood, stopping in at Rutka's father's shoe repair shop, or visiting some of the other small shops that lined the streets of our neighborhood. I remember Baum's green grocery, Szyjowicz's bakery, Stawski's bakery, Nunberg's knockwurst and salami, Regire's pharmacy, and Gipsman's fruit and ice cream shop.

Once in a while, Mother would buy chocolate powder from Gipsman's shop, so beautiful in its small brown cans. Then came one of the great pleasures of my childhood: carefully measuring one heaping teaspoon full of powder, stirring it into a glass of cool milk, and savoring the taste as it flowed over my tongue.

Regire's pharmacy was another magical place; full of row upon row of jars full of strange looking herbs and powders, their vapors mingling to give the whole shop an exotic aroma. Inside, the patrons showed great respect, speaking in lower than normal voices, and taking very much to heart Mr. Regire's advice—Regire said this, or Regire said that. The mystique of this wonderful shop so impressed my little sister Laya that she used to dream of being a pharmacist when she grew up; but sadly, her ambitions would be just a dream.

Next door, Gayleh Rifkeleh, owned another of my favorite places, a bakery and pastry shop. Her cheese cake was legendary, and in the Summer she dispensed the greatest treasure of all–her marvelous ice cream. Gayleh (meaning redhead) was noted for her kindness and generosity, and was much beloved in the community. As her grandson Cvi Cukierman tells us:

"...My Grandmother Gayleh Rifkeleh liked to help all of the people. Every Friday, when we came to her house for Sabbath, Gayleh Rifkeleh asked us to deliver bundles of food she had prepared for people who didn't have enough to eat. She told us to leave the chicken, challah, cakes and other food by the door, not to say who it was from, just to go away, so they would not be embarrassed. This was her practice every week. And it was my job, together with the other grandchildren, to bring these packages to the houses of the needy. Before we had our own meal, my grandmother wanted the others to have their food. She gave to all who needed..."**

Also competing for my affections was Londner's candy store, which was another great place to peer through the panes of the counters and wish, although my cravings to taste his treasures were rarely satisfied.

For seafood we didn't need to leave our house. Rosenblat the fish seller always delivered his fresh fish right to our doorstep. No matter what the time of day or the season, the streets and sidewalks of our neighborhood were always bustling with Jewish people, rich, poor, and in between, hurrying about their business or engaged in endless animated talk. Of course, on the Sabbath there was absolutely no business transacted or even discussed.

I should point out that almost everyone in our neighborhood (as in all neighborhoods) sooner or later acquired a nickname. Once you were labeled, that was how you were referred to from then on. In our family the nicknames went like this (in English translation): Issa was "Chaser of gentile girls"; Moishe, the only one to wear glasses, was "Blind man"; Yossel, who thought a while before he spoke, was "Slow thinker"; Laya, the smallest, was "Shrimp"; and my name was so degrading that I don't want to reveal it.

As a child I very seldom strayed far from my home. The town of Dombrowa Gornicza was little more than a stone throw from Bendzin, but I never went there, not even once. Only on rare occasions, did I tag along with my elders on the streetcar to nearby Sosnowiec, to visit my aunt and uncle and my cousins.

We didn't have a whole lot of entertainment in Bendzin, but we did have a movie theater, so if I begged hard enough, I was allowed to go to a movie. Shirley Temple was definitely my favorite. I convinced myself that we looked very much alike, even though she had curly blond hair and I had straight dark hair, and I just assumed that the two of us shared the same kind of family life and the same Jewish faith.

Bendzin has one very important historic structure which is its castle*, or the Zamek, as we called it, which crowns a rocky summit above a bend in the Czarna (Black) Przemsza River. By the time we inherited it, it was largely in ruins. But even in its degraded state, we could still sense its former grandeur as it stood guard over the wide countryside that lay at its feet.

The city itself was dusty and pretty barren of vegetation, so the Zamek and the area around it were favorite spots for city-weary Bendziners to stroll, picnic, gather chestnuts, and just relax in the soothing greenery. When Rutka and I were old enough to have a little freedom, we would run up the nearby hill to where the ruins of the Zamek stood. We loved to romp and play in the fresh air of the pleasant, green woods that surrounded it. We would kick off our shoes so we could feel the cool grass between our toes, and roll on the ground and let our fantasies run wild. The area immediately around the Zamek had been fenced in as a park, and entrance to the park cost 10 groszen, which was a lot of money for a little girl, so it was a rare treat for us to go into the park and actually play around in the ruins of the Zamek.

Throughout the time I was growing up, ominous storm clouds were gathering around me, but being a small child, I was unaware of such things as Hitler's rise to power in nearby Germany in 1933, and of Germany's growing overt hostility toward my people. In the 1920s and 30s in Poland, the Jewish communities flourished as they never had before. This was a rich, colorful, varied, and unique way of life that had developed in Poland for more than 500 years, and might well be expected to live on for another 500 years and more. No one could imagine that in less than 20 years from the time of my birth, less than 15% of the three and a half million Polish Jews would be alive, and that only a small handful of the survivors would be living in Poland. Today, not one Jew is living in what once was my beloved Bendzin.

The anti-Semitism that pervaded Poland, as well as the rest of Eastern Europe, didn't allow Jews to become fully integrated into the larger society. Our culture was distinct, and we generally lived in our own communities. We spoke our own language (Yiddish), and associated mostly with other Jews. The little contact my parents had with Poles was mostly limited to business transactions. Therefore, I never really thought of myself as Polish, but as Jewish, and despite all that has happened, despite the pain and trauma, despite sometimes feeling abandoned by God, despite it all, I will always be Jewish. As a child I did go to public school, and was taught in the Polish language—for as long as I was able to go to school, which was only until the German invasion.

The school week was followed by my favorite day, the Sabbath, which is called "Shabbat" in Hebrew, but we used the Yiddish form "Shabbes". Shabbes began Friday evening at sunset (officially when three stars were visible in the sky). A few minutes before sunset my mother would conduct the candle lighting ceremony. Covering her head with a scarf, she set two white candles on the table and lit them, then slowly waved her hands over the flames palms down, covered her eyes with her hands and recited the blessing: "Blessed are you, Lord, our God, sovereign of the universe, Who has sanctified us with His commandments and commanded us to light the lights of Shabbat. (Amen)". Some seventy years later, every time either Laya or I perform this little ceremony we picture our mother and remember what a good person she was, and how much we loved her. After the candle lighting, my father and brothers then left for services at the Shul (the synagogue). The evening service began at sundown, and the morning service started at 8 or 9 a.m., beginning with the readings from the Psalms. These prayers were conveniently timed to give stragglers time to get to Shul, for the service proper couldn't start without a minyan present (a quorum of ten adult males). The service usually lasted at least two hours, ending around 9 p.m. Friday night, or about noon on Saturday.

Our Synagogue was strictly Orthodox, as were the vast majority of Polish synagogues which meant that the seating for men and women was separated; therefore, when we went to the synagogue, Mother, Laya, and I simply sat together and prayed, or talked to the other women nearby, but didn't take any active role in the service. We very seldom went except on the High Holidays. Nonetheless, I loved the sense of community that I always felt being in the synagogue, and in the presence of the Holy Ark. As the Ark was opened, the Torah taken out, unwrapped, and carried to the front, I always felt a warm sense of belonging and pride in being a Jew.

On Fridays, extra food had to be prepared, as no work of any kind was allowed to be done from sundown Friday evening until sundown Saturday. We couldn't so much as flip a light switch or tear a piece of paper on Shabbes. For some essential tasks, this taboo was skirted by employing a Gentile to perform the job. For example, when the weather was cold we paid a Polish gentile woman to come in to light a fire in the heating stove.

Of course, Father and my brothers wanted a warm meal when they came home from Shul after morning services, so the Polish woman again came in to warm up the food, which was already cooked the day before. When the men returned, the whole family gathered around the table to enjoy the food.

First Father would wash his hands and recite the Kiddush, the formal sanctification of the day, over a cup of wine. He would then recite the Hamotzi, the blessing of the challah, a loaf of rich white bread leavened with yeast, containing eggs, and braided before baking. From the moment of the ritual washing until after the blessing of the bread, silence reigned in the house. The bread was covered with a cloth challah cover, which was actually a double cover, symbolizing and reminding the household that according to scripture, every Friday while the Israelites were wandering in the desert, a double portion of the miraculous life sustaining food, manna, was given them so they didn't have to gather food on the Sabbath. First, Father held the two challah loaves together with one hand and with his other hand he drew the knife across the loaves in a symbolic cutting gesture, while at the same time reciting the blessing: "Blessed are You, Lord our God, Ruler of the universe, Who brings forth bread from the earth." In unison, the family broke the silence by answering "Amen." Each of us then broke off and ate a small piece of the challah to start the meal.

The Shabbes restrictions did allow for Mother and her daughters to serve the meal. The Shabbes noontime meal always followed the same order of courses: first fish (usually carp), followed by chopped chicken liver, soup (usually chicken noodle), and finally meat (beef, lamb, or chicken) served with carrots. My favorite dish was tshulnt: potatoes with seasoning, onions and some chicken fat, cooked in a covered pot. Our tshulnt was baked in the oven at the bakery, along with the rest of the community's tshulnts, on Friday. Some people made tshulnt with meat, barley other ingredients, and it was the total Shabbes meal. There was a common joke that a good tshulnt gave you enough heart-burn to last until the next Shabbes. The meal ended always with the singing of the Zemirot; sung aloud by the whole family. If a male guest had joined the family for dinner, Father would give him the honor to lead the family in the singing of the Zemirot.

Mealtime was leisurely, as the family talked about many things, such as events of the past week, and events planned for the coming weeks, or months. The only taboo subject was anything financial. For me, the Shabbes meal filled my heart and soul as well as my stomach, and was the best part of being Jewish.

During Pesach (Passover), special dishes were retrieved from the cupboard, which could not be used at any other time of the year. No unleavened bread could be eaten during Pesach, only matzo. One of the delightful side benefits was eating matzo brei, which Mother made by stirring matzo and beaten eggs together and frying them. Mother would scrub the house from top to bottom to assure that not one crumb of bread was left. It is easy to see that our religion was very ritual-centered, and directed every aspect of our lives. This acted as a cement that helped to bond our family together, as it did with the entire Jewish community. Repression by the outside world also created a strong common bond.

*The castle was first built of wood in the mid 13th century, but torn down and rebuilt of stone by Kazimierz the Great around 1358. A few years later, he also built a stone wall around the city for better defense. The castle was partly destroyed and rebuilt several time before its final reconstruction in 1855.

** Ann Weiss, The Last Album—Eyes from the Ashes of Auschwitz-Birkenau; The Jewish Publication Society, Philadelphia

CHAPTER TWO

The Semi-Good Life

The pleasant life I enjoyed with my family continued without interruption through the mid-1930s. I was too young to be concerned about what was happening in Germany, whose border was only a few kilometers away. However, life was not so simple and beautiful for the older members of my family. The newspapers constantly reported on the escalating anti-Semitism happening just across the border. My oldest brother Issa read the paper, and sometimes I overheard him and Father having animated discussions. Politics was a major topic of conversation for my elders, but I had more important concerns, such as how to keep my fingers from freezing when I played in the snow, and how to avoid being smacked by my teacher. Sadly, my childish naïveté would not shield me from the nightmare that was looming in the West.

Around 1935 a big change for the better came to our household. My father bought a real store for selling our shoes, on Kołłantaja Street. No more did we have to operate out of the small back room in our own home, which required the customers to tramp through our living quarters in order to examine the merchandise. The new store had two rooms: a large one where all the shoes could be displayed and examined by many customers at once, and a smaller workroom in the back where my two older brothers, Moishe and Issa, now slept, making so much more room for everybody else at home. In the front of the shop were two large glass display cases facing the street. We filled one case with men's shoes and the other with women's shoes. Since the new store was located in a row of more modern looking one storey shops even the random passerby might discover the shoe store and be tempted to come in and have a look. On one side was Londner's candy store and on the other side a women's undergarment store. Quickly, we began selling more shoes. Since more money was coming in, we were able to move to a larger apartment at #14 Kołłantaja.

Our new apartment building, which housed many more families than the old building, was right across the street from the new store, which made it quite convenient to go back and forth. Our new home, on the second floor, had one less room than the old one, but the rooms were bigger, and we also had an enclosed porch. Entrance to the apartment was up a private stairwell, with its own security door at the top. The whole building shared a common attic as in the previous building, but entrance to the attic was through a different and unconnected stairwell.

The first room we entered at the top of the stairs was the unheated porch, where Yossel slept on a folding bed in the summer months. Behind the porch was the kitchen, which contained a cooking stove, a bed, several large hampers and storage cabinets, and a table. On top of one of the cabinets stood the familiar large water tub, moved over from our old apartment. This kitchen was the main gathering place in the house, where meals were prepared and eaten, books were read, songs were sung, and much of the housework was accomplished. In other words, most of our family life took place in the kitchen.

The door at the back of the kitchen led into the bedroom, the largest room of the apartment. The bedroom was divided by two large wardrobes, with Mother and Father sleeping on one side and Laya and I on the other side. Our new home was heated by a tall, ceramic tiled stove, which stood in the bedroom, and by the cooking stove in the kitchen. When we moved in we didn't have running water in the house, but carried it, bucket by bucket, from a common tap downstairs, and carried out the waste water, bucket by bucket, to the cesspool in the courtyard, just as we had in the old apartment. But before long, my always handy brother Yossel got busy and ran a pipe from the common tap to our apartment. He installed a sink and a toilet in the porch. The toilet was of the type that has the tank near the ceiling and a pull chain. No other family in whole complex had either running water or an indoor toilet in their home. Another huge improvement in our new home, for Mother, was a two-burner kerosene cook stove. Much easier to control than the old coal stove, and no more having to kindle a fire before starting her meals.

We may have had running water and a private toilet, but we, like all of our neighbors and friends, were definitely not rich. In the winter, the food supply was limited and variety was even more limited. We would buy a large sack of potatoes, which were kept frozen solid; an easy thing to do in the Polish winters. The frozen potatoes were peeled and grated, and then combined with egg, hot water, and flour, then molded into a small ball. These balls were boiled in water, and were a major staple of our winter diet, sometimes eaten just boiled, but sometimes fried with a bit of onion. This was our standard meal, which is one more reason why we cherished the Shabbes dinner.

Frugality was a way of life. I don't remember ever seeing a store that sold ready-made clothes. For dresses, Mother would buy material by the yard and take it to a dressmaker. The men had their clothes made by a tailor. There were a great many tailors in Bendzin, and they all worked very hard, but very few could be called prosperous. Unless you were the eldest son or daughter, you seldom got new clothes; you had to be happy with hand-me-downs, somewhat refurbished as necessary. My poor little sister Laya complains to this day about never having a new dress. She says, "Everything was Dora, Dora, Dora—Laya was nothing; she didn't even exist."

I believe it was sometime in 1938 that a very unpleasant, and I assume, unexpected affair shook the family. Mother's brother Shloimo who had been raised by my parents as their own child, and whom I had always thought of as my oldest brother, left the family shoe store, and opened a shoe store of his own. The galling thing about this was that he opened the store just a couple of doors down from ours, and with money which he had apparently been "borrowing" from the family business for some time. We were sure of this, as we knew he had no large supply of funds of his own. After that we all avoided Shloimo like the plague, even to the point of crossing the street to avoid walking past his store. Mother was especially hurt and embittered by his lack of loyalty; after all, she had raised him as her own child from a baby. Why he pulled this dirty trick, I don't know; perhaps he never felt that Father treated him the same as his own sons; who knows?

In 1933, I started public school in the Podlinska School. Even though Piłsudski was still alive, the Polish government had eliminated school subsidies for Jewish schools, with the result that all but the richest Jewish children throughout Poland attended public schools, with the classes taught in Polish, rather than in Yiddish which was spoken at home. Perhaps the government hoped that the Jews would either assimilate or emigrate. In addition to reading and writing (in Polish) and arithmetic, we had PE, and singing.

All Jewish boys received extensive training in Judaism and the Hebrew language from a very young age at what was called the Kheyder. Most families, like mine, also felt that girls should also have some education in these matters; so in the afternoon, after I had been to public school, I was sent to the Bais Yaakov School in Bendzin.* Although I liked the teacher and enjoyed my time there, downstairs from the school was a big dog that barked ferociously at me every time I went up the stairs to the school; this terrified me so much that I dreaded going to school, but my parents insisted that I must go. In fact my education was so important to my parents that they hired a private tutor for me when I was too sick to go to school.

Every school day, I was up at 7 a.m. for a breakfast of milk or hot chocolate with bread and butter, and usually an egg as well. Public school lasted from 8 a.m. to 2 p.m., with a break for lunch. I always took a sack lunch from home, which was usually just a bread and butter sandwich, but occasionally I was lucky enough to get my very favorite treat—salami. I walked to school every day, about 15 minutes, passing by a small city park, which boasted a few trees and a few benches. There were about 20 students in my class, almost all of them Jewish. All the kids had to wear a uniform to school–a black dress with a white collar for the girls. It seemed that I could never get my collar white enough to please my fastidious teacher, who often sent me home with strict instructions to get the collar whiter. No matter how much I scrubbed and scrubbed, and bleached and starched that collar, I never really succeeded in getting it white enough to satisfy this teacher.

Mostly the teacher conducted the class like a bunch of automatons, repeating our lessons in unison. In other words, learning was, except for math, largely a matter of rote memorization. Discipline was very, very strict. Most of the teachers were like no-nonsense drill sergeants. Since I had one bad eye, I always had to sit up front so I could see the blackboard better, and sitting on the front row made me more vulnerable. If you got caught not paying attention, or giggling, or whispering to a friend, you could expect a smart slap on the palm with a ruler. If that didn't straighten you out, the teacher embarrassed you by sitting you in the corner facing the wall for the rest of the class period. Finally, if you hadn't learned to behave yourself, they would make you sit outside the schoolhouse. The outside punishment was especially effective in winter; sitting out in the snow and wind usually persuaded the most unruly student to change his or her behavior. Whether or not it made them feel that they were in the wrong and the teacher was right is another question. Our schoolhouse was not insulated, but nonetheless, it was a lot colder outside than inside, making discipline easier to maintain in winter than in spring. Generally speaking, the warmer it got, the harder it was for the teacher to keep order in the classroom.

In my class I was one of the difficult cases, often being caught talking and, or giggling in class. One time the teacher sent me home with a letter to my parents detailing my supposed high crimes. On receiving this report, in spite of my pleadings of innocence, Father took his belt to me. I didn't even get to call my lawyer. Corporal punishment at home, and at school, was quite acceptable in those days. It was also the norm for the father of the family to be the "King of his castle," and my father didn't hesitate to assert his authority. Sometimes he was quite abusive, not only to me, but to Mother and Issa, as well. That is, until one day a nearly grown-up Issa firmly told Father that he had better not lay a finger again on himself or Mother. When he whipped me this time he explained to me that the reason he punished me, was that it was part of Jewish tradition to set a good example for the rest of the world, and I should never forget that. It soon became apparent, however, that the rest of the world had no appreciation for any good behavior by me or any other Jew.

One day, part way into the second grade at school, I began to feel really sick as the day ground on. Struggling to stay upright in my chair, and hoping that I wouldn't be called on, I barely managed to last out the day. I walked home bent over double from a pain that kept getting worse. Sometimes it was in my stomach, but sometimes it seemed to come from my back, or my legs, or from just all over my entire body.

As soon as I got home, I fell in a groaning heap on the floor beneath Mother's horrified gaze. What followed went like this:

"Dora! What's wrong?" Mother screamed.

"I don't know," I answered weakly. "I don't feel good."

"Where does it hurt?"

"My stomach, my back, I don't know, everywhere."

After tenderly putting me to bed, Mother ran out, saying, "I'm going to get Dr. Szer."

Dr. Szer wasn't really a doctor with a medical degree, but a "house doctor," or "Felcher", who visited sick people in their homes rather than having an office. He had no diploma, but was well versed in dispensing home remedies and folk wisdom. Sometimes his patients got better; sometimes they didn't. Not really much different from the results obtained by the more expensive doctors who had offices in town. As far as I know, the town had only one real Doctor, Dr. Weinziher, and only the well-to-do could afford to see him.

Herman Szer was a man of average build, in his late thirties, sporting a narrow black mustache –of the type favored by many men of the times, including Charlie Chaplin and one Adolf Hitler. He took himself very seriously, and always dressed very neatly in a black suit and black derby, and carried a black medicine bag. Herman always charged three złotys per visit, no matter what he did. Of course, he charged whether the patient got better or not, and he was very persistent in collecting his fee.

His favorite cure, which was a popular one for that time, was to find the apparent location of the problem and then heat bainkas (small glass cups) with his little alcohol burner. When hot, he would place these heated bainkas on the afflicted area, where they would stick from suction, later leaving a red ring on the skin when they fell off. This treatment, however popular, was only rarely effective. When someone was asked if some action was helpful, the reply was often, "Helfen vi a toyten bainkas", ("As helpful as bainkas on a dead man.")

I was still lying miserably on my bed three hours later when the house doctor arrived. He had no instruments, but conducted his examination by looking, listening, and feeling.

"She has a very high fever. Have you used the bathroom today?"

"I can't."

"Why not?"

"I can't."

"Give her some parsley soup without salt, and I'll check back in the morning."

After the doctor left, Mother made up the parsley soup and also some chicken soup, carefully leaving out the salt. I refused to eat either soup, but Mother forced a little bit of the chicken soup down my throat. Mother was so concerned that I might not live, that she went to the cemetery, as was the Jewish custom, and prayed at the stones of her family that they should help me survive.

The next day, by the time the doctor came around in the morning, as promised, I couldn't even talk.

"How is she?"

"She's even worse than yesterday."

"Did she eat any soup?"

"I was only able to force a couple of spoons of chicken soup down her throat."

"What would you like to eat?" the doctor asked me.

I just lay there, too weak to answer him.

"Can you talk?"

I couldn't answer him, of course.

"Well, even if you can't talk, can you shake your head yes or no?"

I shook my head, yes.

"OK," the Felcher said in triumph.   "Would you like some bread?"

I shook my head no.

"How about some chicken soup?" I shook my head no again.

The doctor turned to Mother and asked. "What will she eat?"

Mother's thoughtful reply was, "If she will eat anything it would be salami, but you know, it has a lot of salt.

"Well, we have nothing to lose. We've got to get her to eat something."

Smiling, he leaned over close to me and asked, "Would you like some salami?"

This time I nodded my head, yes. Mother and the Felcher exchanged a grateful smile. It was the first time my mother had smiled since I came home from school the day before. She cut me a thin slice of salami, which I had no trouble in eating, and with the outlook much better, Dr. Szer collected his three złotys, put on his derby, and took his leave. Slowly, I began to get better, and for the rest of my life I've often said, "Salami saved my life."

It took five months for me to get well enough to go back to school. The principal told my parents that I had missed too much of the year, and they would have to hold me back and have me repeat the second grade. I couldn't bear the thought of this, and I threatened suicide, not out of any concern over my academic career, but because being held back would separate me from my best friend Rutka. Of course, I lost the battle, and from then on I was a year older than my classmates. But each day after school I continued to play with my beloved Rutka who remained loyal, despite my lower status in school.

A year or so later, my poor constitution led to another bout with sickness. This time, for some unknown reason, I was unable to walk. Dr. Szer resorted to one of his most drastic home remedies –the pigskin treatment. This involved wrapping my feet in pigskin. For Jews to resort to using anything to do with pigs, it must have had good results for many people, but for me this disgusting, sticky, and smelly treatment had no beneficial effect at all, so the family decided that their only hope was to take me on the long bus journey to the health spa town of Busko Zdroj—about fifty miles northeast of Krakow. People from all over Europe came (and still do) to Busko Zdroj to "take the waters," and parboil in the various mineral-water baths and mud baths. The hot springs waters contain sulfides, bromides, iodides, and selenium in various combinations, which are drunk, gargled, or soaked in, depending upon the affliction being treated. The doctors at the spa didn't give you free rein to just jump into the baths. You were thoroughly examined, and given a specific regimen, with exact time to be spent in each bath spelled out. I would say that the whole works were applied to me. After two weeks of this regimen, the treatments worked–I could walk again. Mother joyfully wrote back to the rest of the family about my marvelous recovery, and of our plans to return home. When I got back home, I was given a big hug and kiss from everybody in the family.

Once my health returned, Mother took me to my grandfather Szpringer's house in Zharki, only about 25 miles away as the crow flies, but a two hour bumpy ride as the bus goes. Zharki was one of a myriad of shtetls – primarily Jewish villages—scattered across Eastern Europe. These shtetls gave the world a unique, vibrant, colorful culture. There were also many gentiles living in these towns, and they, more or less, lived in peaceful co-existence with the Jews, until the war came.

I saw my Grandfather only a few times, and being a small child, I don't remember very much about him, except that he was very old, rail-thin, had a long white beard, and dressed in the garb of a religious Jew. When they were raising their family, Grandfather and Grandmother Gitel shared a very small, crude one-room house with their six children, including my father. Grandfather's workshop was also crowded into this room. This one room contained a bed, a table and a small cooking stove, which doubled as a room heater. This sort of cramped living condition was normal for all but the rich. By the time I visited them the children were grown, and had moved out, but Grandfather and his new wife still lived in the old house.

There was no running water in the house and of course no toilet. Water had to be pumped and carried from the well in the middle of the village, which supplied all the homes. Scattered around were various small family shops—one for bread, one for meat, and so on.

When we visited, we didn't want to crowd into Grandfather's little home, so we rented a room in another house in the forest, about a quarter of a mile away. In Zharki I loved to walk in the huge surrounding quiet, green forest and to go swimming and splashing in the wonderful pond not far from Grandfather's house. The pond was fed by a delightful spring with clean, cold drinking water. Several of my aunts and uncles lived nearby, so I always had plenty of cousins to play with. It seemed like every time I went there, I met new ones I had never seen before.

Overall, our life in Bendzin was a good life mainly because of the love and solidarity within our family, and also the sense of belonging we got from our Jewish Faith and community. Our life of frugality in rough living conditions was just something that we accepted as normal and necessary. One thing we could not accept as necessary was the anti-Semitism that had existed in Poland and throughout Eastern Europe for centuries, and which we faced on an almost daily basis. Occasionally, some Jew would be hit or even beaten up in the street for no reason, other than his being a Jew. Occasionally we were subjected to pogroms, usually minor in Bendzin, with thugs rampaging through the Jewish district, smashing store windows, looting, and beating up any Jew unfortunate enough to be caught outside. We usually had sufficient warning in time to board up the store and keep low until the storm passed. As the 1930s went on, even killings of Jews became more common. In such cases, there was less and less recourse to the law. The situation grew worse after 1935, when Jozeph Piłsudski died, and with his death, feelings of anti-Semitism that had been only barely restrained before, quickly came to the surface throughout Poland. In practicality, the Jews had no particular rights.

However, the Jews were not always passive. On one occasion in 1936 or 1937, our community got word that a large group of Poles planned to loot our stores, and would be entering Bendzin by crossing the bridge over the Czarna Przemsza River. When this group of anti-Semitic thugs arrived at the bridge, carrying big sacks in anticipation of hauling home a sizable quantity of ill-gotten booty, they were quite surprised to be confronted by a determined contingent of burly Jewish workmen. In the ensuing scrap the Jews sent the Poles running home with their tails between their legs, many of them being knocked out and thrown off the bridge into the river.

As a child, I didn't understand all of this discrimination, but I soon learned that it was part of being a Jew. As the '30's moved toward the '40's, while changes in the laws and actions in Germany against Jews were dramatic, changes in Polish laws and practices, which steadily diminished our rights, seemed comparatively slight. They seemed to be just minor cycles in a larger eternal pattern, like a harsh or a mild winter. We had no choice but to go about our lives and hope for better times ahead.

But not all Jews were willing to sit passively, and wait for things to get better, particularly the young people. Issa had joined a Zionist organization dedicated to moving Jews to Palestine. His was just one of many activist groups in Bendzin. In fact, Bendzin was loaded with brash, brave young Jewish men and women. The state of Israel didn't exist yet–but the gathering of the Jewish people in our ancient homeland was already underway. Issa even went to a training camp in a nearby town to make preparations for the planned journey to Palestine. Unfortunately, the German invasion quashed these plans.

Like Issa, Moishe also wanted to find a new life abroad. He filled out the proper application forms and after some considerable delay, he was informed that he had permission to emigrate to Venezuela. Permission gained was a big hurdle, but that still left many problems. Who would pay for the move? What would he do when he got there? What would happen to the rest of the family who stayed behind in Poland? The net result was that the practical and logistical problems associated with a trans-Atlantic move were simply too much, and Moishe's plan to leave Poland fell through for lack of motivation and money. As events proved, of course, moving anywhere outside of Poland would have been a wise move for any Jew, at any price and effort.

*Prior to 1917 it was not common for young Jewish girls to get much schooling in Judaism. Recognizing this need, Sarah Schenirer, a seamstress in Krakow, founded the Bais Yaakov movement, which spread throughout Poland and eventually the rest of the world.

CHAPTER THREE

Invasion

Anyone who thought about it at all, realized that the eastern part of Upper Silesia, which had been hungrily coveted by both Germany and Czechoslovakia for years, was potentially a prime target for German expansion. German influence was already well established in this region, and unless the glorious Polish army could match the Germans' tanks with their horse cavalry, there was nothing to stop the Germans from quickly adding the balance of Upper Silesia, with its riches in natural resources, to the expanding Reich. This was of course exactly what would happen, but no one, except maybe the Germans, would have believed how extremely quickly the Germans would gobble up all of Poland. The whole world was to learn a lesson in modern warfare and what "blitzkrieg" meant.

Because I wasn't politically savvy as a young girl, the war sort of sneaked up on me, but as I mentioned before, the older members of my family had kept themselves well informed about all the events that might impact our lives, so they weren't taken too much by surprise when the German invasion did come. However, nobody could comprehend, or would have believed, what diabolical plans the Nazis had for the Polish Jews. So, while the Germans were busily preparing for their invasion, Moishe, Issa, and Father were busy in Bendzin running the shoe store and trying to convince themselves that whatever was going on in Germany would stay in Germany. Mother had her hands full taking care of her family, and managing the books and paperwork of the store, because Father could neither read nor write Polish. Since the store was a small operation, Yossel was working outside the family business, in a building supply and hardware store. Laya and I were still children of 10 and 12 years of age.

Having no way of knowing when, where, or even if, the war would start, in late August Mother packed a few things, and with her daughters in hand, headed for Busko Zdroj, as she had done every year since my earlier illnesses. This was indeed a well earned vacation, where she could relax by just resting, or by strolling among the splendid flower beds and shady trees. What a relief this was from the toil of housework in the heat, noise, and dust of Bendzin. But this year our pleasant vacation was cut short by a surprise visit from Yossel. He had rushed from Bendzin to warn us that war might break out at any time, and we should come back home at once. In Busko we had no telephone, or any other news source, so we had been blissfully ignorant of events taking place in the world outside. We immediately packed and caught the next bus home, arriving there only a day or so before the Blitzkrieg struck.

As soon as the war began, Father and Mother agreed that it would be wise for the females in the family to hide out in a rural area before the war reached Bendzin. It was decided that Yossel should escort his mother and sisters to Szczekociny, a small city some 40 to 50 miles northeast of Bendzin on the banks of the Pilica River, where about half of its 5600 citizens were Jews. Mother's cousin Szmul lived there and we hoped we could stay with him until things settled down. So the four of us packed a few necessities, and climbed aboard a bus headed for, we hoped, a safer place. Issa also, along with many of his youth group, had taken off for parts unknown to the east. These young men had no desire to be drafted into the Polish army. Therefore, Moishe and Father were the only family members who stayed in Bendzin to keep an eye on our house and the store, and to face the Germans when they showed up. So, for the first time, our family was split up, a pattern that was to be repeated many times, with the result that we soon wouldn't even know if any of the others were even alive.

We were not the only ones to flee the city; from what we understand, the majority of the Bendzin Jews also left. They reasoned, as we did, that if they found some smaller town to take refuge in, they might escape the expected bombing and shelling. Thousands upon thousands of people from towns to the west, Poles and Jews alike, carrying what they could of their possessions, came trudging through Bendzin to escape the war zone. Most of them drifted back home after things quieted down.

Upon arrival in Szczekociny, we were warmly greeted by Szmul and his wife, who were as nervous as we were about the advancing Wehrmacht (the German Armed Forces). Cousin Szmul not only had a safer location in a rural area, he also had a hiding place already prepared in the basement, with a hidden trap door for an entrance. After all, these were Jews in Poland where anti-Semitism had been a reality for hundreds of years, so they were prepared for any emergency. We weren't there more than a few days, before the rumble of artillery shells exploding could clearly be heard in the distance, like an approaching thunder storm. Although we hadn't seen any Germans yet, the explosions were definitely getting louder as the hours passed. We all agreed that it would be prudent to abandon the idea of hiding in the basement, and to move on to an even smaller village to the east. A bus was out of the question, so we hurriedly procured a horse and wagon, loaded a few provisions and ourselves aboard, and headed down the road. Even after Szczekociny had receded from view, we continued to look back, and could now observe plumes of dense black smoke ascending from what we hoped, for cousin Szmul's sake, wasn't our recent refuge. Our new destination was the village of Wodzislaw, about 17 km. as the crow flies, but many jolting hours away by horse and wagon, where cousin Szmul had some friends.

In Wodzislaw, our new hosts, although surprised by this wagon load of refugees, graciously invited us to share their modest farmhouse. The first night passed uneventfully, and no shelling could be heard. All of the children slept crosswise in the one bed. Everybody else slept on the floor. The next morning the situation grew more frightening. We had no idea what to expect; no one had seen any Germans yet–but the unmistakable announcements of their impending arrival were increasingly plain for all to hear. The explosions were getting closer and closer. Everyone in the village was nervous and frightened with no certain idea of what action to take. As there was clearly no place to escape to, there really was no choice except to stay put. Beneath most houses was a windowless cellar, which would give protection from anything but a direct hit. Most of the villagers did what we did, which was to crouch in the cellar and pray. Outside we could hear artillery shells exploding and rifle shots being fired, and then suddenly all went quiet. While we were cowering in the cellar wondering what we should do next, the answer came in the form of a motorcycle with sidecar screeching into the yard, manned by two German soldiers.

The driver turned off the engine and his boots could be heard crunching across gravel of the yard. In a loud and commanding voice the German ordered all the men in the cellar to come out with their hands up. Getting no response, the German repeated his order in a louder and more demanding voice. Having no other choice, Yossel, Szmul, and the farmer went outside and were taken away, for what seemed like an eternity. Time passes slowly when you are sitting in the dark in a damp cellar. When Yossel came back, he told us we could all come out. He had been taken to the village square along with the other men from the village, but none of them had been harmed. Standing at the water pump in the yard was another German soldier in his neat but dusty field-gray uniform, handing out candy to the children. This soldier's courteous and non-threatening manner led us to hope that perhaps our fears of the Germans were exaggerated. Mother walked over to him and asked him what we should do. He said we should remain right where we were, and after things quieted down we could all return to our homes. He didn't seem to know himself when that might be. He and his passenger soon mounted their iron horse and roared away in a cloud of dust.

We were all anxious to go home, but since the Germans were constantly passing by in their trucks, motorcycles, and tanks, we knew we would have to stay put for a few more days. It was obvious that the Polish army wasn't doing too well. In fact, none of us ever saw a single Polish soldier in the whole time we were away from Bendzin. Eventually, we went back to Szczekociny, where we found most of the houses completely destroyed. Cousin Szmul's house was only slightly damaged, but it had been thoroughly looted. All his possessions of any value were gone. So after several more days of nervous waiting, Mother, Yossel, Laya, and I rented another horse and buggy and took the slow road back to Bendzin, to face the unknown, grim reality that would confront us.

Having a long history of being run over by armies from all directions, both Polish and Jewish citizens knew that although the war would be fought by soldiers, the civilians would be caught in the middle of the conflict, and would suffer greatly. Remembering World War I, the government issued the citizens so-called "gas masks," which were actually just a white piece of cloth. In a way, these so-called gas masks symbolized the whole situation. The masks were as ineffective and outmoded as the Polish army, which was decades behind the times.

My father wasn't a man who liked to rely on hope, but after Yossel and the female members of the household left, all that he and Moishe could do was to brace themselves for the inevitable arrival of the Germans, and then take whatever actions they could to protect our home and the precious family's store.

In Bendzin, the Polish army had arrived shortly after the invasion, and set up a few machine gun emplacements pointed down the road to Czeladz, to the west, and then blew up the bridge over the Czarna Przemsza River. Unfortunately, the Polish machine guns were all pointed the wrong way, as the Germans arrived from the south. Furthermore, the river under the bridge that they blew up could be waded across. As soon as the Germans arrived, the Polish army disappeared without firing a single shot, and so, on September 4th, 1939 the mighty forces of the Master Race vanquished little Bendzin. Polish citizens lined the streets with cheers, as the arrogant conquerors paraded down the main streets of my hometown, and girls ran out to toss flowers to them and kiss the soldiers. I'm sure that a great many of the Poles were thinking, "Now maybe we can get rid of the Goddamned Jews."

On that same day these Supermen murdered 90 helpless Jews in my father's home shtetl of Zharki.

CHAPTER FOUR

Subjugation and Atrocities

One of the first acts of the Germans was to rename the city Bendsburg, and then post a printed bulletin all over town, written in German, Polish and Yiddish, stating as follows:

To All the Jews:
All the Jews of all ages, both men and women, are required to register immediately with the Jewish Council. The Jews failing to obey this order will be refused ration cards, and will be prosecuted.

The German text was signed by Bendzin's new German mayor, and the Yiddish text was signed by the new German-appointed boss of the Jewish population, Moniek (Moishe) Merin. In Bendzin, the Germans used the same pattern they followed throughout Poland. The Germans created a Jewish Council, or Judenrat, and placed most of the burden of running the affairs of the Jews on that council. Of course, these Jewish "leaders" on the Judenrat were completely under the thumb of their German masters. As the enforcement arm of the Judenrat they created a Jewish police force, called the "Melitz" by the Jewish citizens. The Melitz had the task of doing all of the dirty work for the Judenrat, who were following orders handed to them by the Germans. It follows that the Melitz really served the Germans, not the Jews. The Melitz were generally hated by the rest of the Jews, but we realized that the men who joined, did so in the hope of saving the lives of their own families. It is uncomfortable to ask yourself, "What would I do in the same circumstances?"

However, there were many in the Melitz who went well beyond what was necessary in the use of force, even to the point of brutality.

The Germans got great delight out of watching Jews being beaten up by other Jews, but in the end they showed these perpetrators no more mercy than they showed the rest of us.

Although being a member of the Judenrat yielded many advantages over their charges, their lot was far from being totally enviable. These leaders were placed in the impossible position of attempting to please the Germans and the Jews at the same time. Most of them struggled to do what they could for the people in their charge, but ultimately they had to please the Germans completely, regardless of the consequences to the Jews they were supposed to help. This naturally led to their being increasingly hated by the other Jews. If they balked at carrying out the Germans' wishes, they would be removed from their position, and might be transported (sent to a concentration camp), or even executed, or if lucky, simply lowered to the status of an ordinary person.

Just two days after the Germans marched in, all Jews of Bendzin were ordered to assemble at 10 a.m. on September 6th, with a follow-up meeting set for noon. A huge crowd gathered at 10 a.m. to hear Moniek Merin complain petulantly that although he was "in charge," no one was listening to him. At noon, Merin announced that the Germans had demanded that the Jews deliver 5 kilograms of gold to them by noon the next day. Merin dramatically took the gold ring off his finger and placed it on the table in front of him. He then exhorted all the others to do likewise, as the only way to save themselves from the wrath of the Germans. He passed along the promise the Germans had made to him, that if they met this demand the Germans would be merciful to them. In his speech he said:

"There is only one holy aim before us: to save our lives from the fire burning around us, for we are enclosed in a death-ring. Let us ransom ourselves with our gold. Let our money atone for our lives."

It is impossible to know now if he himself believed what he was saying. What is sure is that some in the crowd believed him and the gold was gathered and turned over, but of course, the Germans' promise was a farce.

Moniek was a slender man in his late thirties, but looked only about 25. Before the war, he had been a commercial broker. He was separated from his wife and led a bachelor's life, spending a lot of time in coffee houses, playing cards and billiards, always for money, which he almost always lost. He had always felt that he was destined for a greater role in life. And he was right; in spite of all his efforts to ingratiate the enemy, less than four years later, Merin himself would end up standing in front of a firing squad at Auschwitz's infamous "black wall."

With the initial invasion accomplished and the war front moved on to the east, Bendzin changed from a war zone to an occupied zone. With typical German efficiency, it took very little time for them to establish new laws to control our lives.

First of all, a dusk to dawn curfew was imposed, with severe consequences for anyone violating it. Next, everyone was required to have an identification book, issued by the Germans. Each book, written in Polish and German, had the holder's fingerprint, the person's name, address, profession, and most importantly for the Nazis, his or her religion, and was stamped with a swastika (we called it a haknkreyts—crooked cross). Every individual was warned that he, or she, must be able to produce this ID at a moment's notice, when so demanded by any German. Failure to produce the papers would result in a trip to the police station, where the offending party would be put under a magnifying glass. One had better have a good excuse for not having valid papers; culpable Jews often found themselves on the next transport to a slave labor camp, or after January, 1942, most likely to Auschwitz.

Another requirement was that everything was rationed, and every family was issued ration cards. The lines stretched endlessly and many people never even made it to the front before the shop closed for the day. It became a routine for every member of the family to get up at 3 a.m. to go stand in various lines for the most basic necessities, such as food and fuel. Families with several children to act as line-standers had an advantage, for there were many lines to obtain the necessities of life. Of course, the downside was, the more children, the more mouths to feed. Hence life for many became simply standing in line all day and accomplishing nothing else. This was true for both Poles and Jews; however the Jews had another problem. Often when a Jew was in line with Poles, some Poles would push him to the end of the line, so that he might never make it to the front. Or even worse, when an SS man was nearby, some Pole would catch his attention by pointing to the Jew and yelling, "Jew, Jew!"

Resulting in the hapless Jew being pulled out of the line, to be kicked and beaten, giving many of the Poles something to laugh about.

All businesses, including Jewish, had to be kept open, and services were to be maintained as before the occupation. Secondly, the Germans also ordered that all prices must be kept the same as before the invasion—not one grosz higher. We were warned that if we did not comply, the store would be broken open and all the merchandise thrown into the street. Being ordered to keep the store open sounded good to us, and we willingly complied. These were minor problems, but the Nazis wasted little time, just five days from entering our town, to reveal what their real plans were for us.

On the pleasant summer evening of September 9, 1939, the Nazis launched their dedicated campaign of murder and torture against us, the Jews of Bendzin, and the ravaging persisted for another four years, until these self- appointed Supermen were satisfied that not one single Jew was left alive in our city. Their murderous crusade was inaugurated with an unmistakable message. Less than a five minute walk from our home, on Bozniczna Street, stood the main Synagogue of Bendzin, one of the finest synagogues in all of Poland, and was the pride of our community. Few onlookers survived to testify as to what they witnessed that day. The SS, assisted by German soldiers, rounded up at least 200 Jewish men, at random, forced them into the synagogue, chained the doors shut, and set the building on fire. As they listened to the screams coming from inside the synagogue, the only concern the Nazis had was that not one of these fellow human beings would escape alive. They were completely successful, as only the screams of the victims escaped from the inferno. When the last pitiful pleadings of those poor souls inside the synagogue were replaced by only the crackling of the flames, the Nazis still hadn't sated their thirst for murder, so they moved their attention to the adjacent buildings, mostly multi-family houses.

A several block area, home to hundreds of Jewish families, was surrounded by the killers, and all of the buildings were torched by throwing gasoline on them and igniting it with hand grenades thrown in to speed up the process. Stunned and bewildered, the occupants poured out into the courtyards, mostly dressed in their night clothes, but there was no escape, as the front entrances had been barred with heavy chains to prevent evacuation. Those who frantically attempted to jump out of windows from the burning homes were coolly shot by the soldiers and SS. Those who succeeded in escaping the flaming buildings were picked off as they attempted to run away. Many people were shot for trying to help the victims. Some were shot for simply being out on the street and not finding an escape route quickly enough. Mostly they were shot at close range—a bullet in the head, a bullet in the head, a bullet in the head. During this nighttime atrocity an estimated 56 houses were burned down, and hundreds of helpless men, women, and children died horrible deaths. Among the houses torched that night was the home I was born in—the one we had luckily moved out of a couple of years before. Bendzin was not singled out as the only city to be the victim of this type of atrocity. Synagogues in many towns were torched with helpless, innocent people locked inside to be reduced to ashes. This savage night of barbarism was orchestrated by rational men from what was supposedly one of the most civilized countries on the planet.

These Jews who perished that night, like the vast majority of the three million Polish Jews who were murdered in the Holocaust, did not receive any miracle, and whatever astute choices they may have made prior to that day were all nullified. Instead they found themselves in a situation where there was no way to resist, no place to run to, and no place to hide. It was simply luck – or if you prefer, a miracle –undeserved, unplanned, unexplainable–that none of our family were ever caught in this position. But still, we tend to believe that our survival was also aided by many choices made

by various members of the family, which reduced the odds of our
getting into such a hopeless situation.

When Mother, Yossel, Laya, and I returned to Bendzin from
Szczekociny, and Issa came home from wherever he was hiding,
none of us had any knowledge of the horrible atrocities that had
just been inflicted on the city. A pall hung over the town, accented
by the still smoldering remains of our Synagogue and the homes
of our friends and neighbors. Besides the physical change, there
was palpable fear in everybody's eyes and the sounds of mourning
coming from inside of homes. Father gave us the tragic account
of how, while we were gone, the Nazis had packed the Jews into
the synagogue, and burned it to the ground with the Jews inside.
No one had escaped. He described for us the mass burning of the
houses and the carnage in the streets. He described the screams of
those burning to death. It was too horrible for us to believe, but we
believed it. We now understood that look in the eyes of our fellow
Jews in the streets of Bendzin. Our city was just one of most of the
cities and towns in Poland and the rest of Eastern Europe where
the synagogue was burned down, often with Jews locked inside.

Shortly after coming back to Bendzin, Issa left again; this time
to seek refuge in Russia.

Anti-Semitism with its curses and mistreatment was one thing
everyone was used to. Discrimination at school and in profession-
al life was common. But not since 1648 during the uprisings of
Bogdan Khmelnitski, when as many as 100,000 Jews were slaughtered in the most barbarous fashion, had such large groups of
Jews been so cruelly murdered just for being Jews. Incidentally, to
this day Khmelnitski is a great national hero in the Ukraine.

It was abundantly clear what the Third Reich had in mind for
the Jews of Poland. Day after day the killings continued, on a less-
er scale, sometimes randomly and sometimes in a cold-bloodedly
calculated fashion. The morning after the synagogue and home
burnings, a young man trying to say Kaddish for the dead was shot
in the head, right in the street as he prayed. He was a friend of
Moishe's and only 19 years old. Even the baker, Mr. Stawski, from
whom we had bought our bread since we could remember, was
hanged in public. He had been denounced to the Nazis by some

Polish woman, and found guilty of the unpardonable crime of charging one grosz too much for a loaf of bread. As a warning to rest of the populace, a note to this effect was pinned to his body for all to read as his corpse dangled from the gallows.

Although the brunt of the terror was directed toward the Jews, the gentile Poles were not being given a free ride. In one of their unexplainable actions, the day after the burning of the synagogue, the Nazis rounded up 30 Poles whom they accused of burning the synagogue and the nearby homes. These 30 Poles were hanged or shot in the public square to set an example, of what, one can only guess. Perhaps they wanted the Poles to know that the Nazis wanted to reserve the pleasure of killing Jews for themselves. Most Poles weren't broken-hearted to see the synagogue burned, but nobody, Jew or Pole, was fooled as to the identity of the real perpetrators of this hideous crime.

After sundown boisterous groups of German soldiers wandered the city, singing German songs and terrorizing anyone who came into their path, however innocently. Residents would go to sleep in fear–many were hardly able to sleep because with increasing frequency, groups of soldiers would burst into random houses with no warning in the middle of the night, taking whatever and whomever they pleased. Day or night, it wasn't uncommon for soldiers to stop a person on the street and rob him, beat him up, or even shoot him.

For any German soldier who was sadistic by nature, the Jews, especially in Eastern Europe, were an abundant and easily accessible resource, to play out his cruelest fantasies. I'm referring primarily to those stationed behind the battle front. No one would inhibit any German from committing the most barbarous of crimes. To the contrary, in a great many situations, the willingness to commit atrocities would be rewarded by promotion. My family and I were subjected to a nightmarish spectacle, early one morning, right outside our own window.

The strict enforcement of the curfew offered a perfect excuse for any sadistic Nazi to practice his cruelty. Downstairs across the courtyard Jacob Martin and his wife Jadza lived with their three sons and two daughters. Every morning and evening Jacob would go out to the edge of town, where some people kept a few cows, to buy fresh milk, and bring it home to sell to the neighbors. They would chill the milk in their home, and each morning, Jadza would go out, wearing a huge shawl to cover the milk, and peddle it to her neighbors. We always bought our milk from her.

This ill-fated morning, Jadza opened the big door to the street, carrying her pitcher of milk, meant for someone down the street. Unfortunately, she was observed by a German soldier patrolling with his dog. Checking his watch he saw that it was a minute or two before the end of curfew. Relishing the opportunity to show the Jews that their Master's orders must be strictly obeyed, this Nazi immediately seized Jadza and dragged her back inside the common courtyard. In the middle of the courtyard was a communal waste water drain. The Nazi then grabbed her and violently shoved her headlong into the drain pit. He then began kicking her while the excited dog circled around viciously biting her; then setting his booted foot on the back of her neck, this depraved soldier began beating her with his rifle butt, while his canine accomplice ferociously ripped at her legs. Jadza was soon rendered unconscious, but neither the beating nor the biting ceased. Only when this Nazi had sated his lust for brutality did he abandon his attack. Not until this Aryan hero had proudly strutted out the front door with his faithful companion trotting at his side, could poor Jadza's family rush out and carry their bruised and bleeding wife and mother back inside her home. At the first sounds of his yelling and her pleading, we all rushed to the window, but knowing the danger of being observed, we furtively peered through the curtains at the terrible scene. I imagine the whole apartment complex was watching in horror, but anyone attempting to help Jadza would have been shot on the spot. By the end of the war, Jacob, Jadza, and their five children would all be murdered by the Nazis.

Very soon after occupation, trucks manned by soldiers cruised the streets at random during the day. Often, if an individual or a small group of Jews would be out on the street when a truck passed, the truck would stop; a couple of soldiers would dismount from the back and prod the unfortunate citizens into the truck with their bayonets. Protesting only resulted in a bruising blow by a rifle butt. The people thus Shanghaied off the street were generally sent to a labor camp. Under these conditions, it isn't surprising that fewer and fewer people went out of their houses unnecessarily, and when they did so they went as quickly possible. When the roving trucks could find no people on the streets, they frequently stopped in front of a house or apartment, stormed inside, and simply abducted anyone who suited their needs and herded them outside into the waiting trucks. Of course, no one dared to be out during the dusk to dawn curfew.

Before long, this random method of "recruiting" workers gave way to a much more efficient scheme—efficiency being a hallmark of any German operation. This crude method also required the use of many soldiers who could be better utilized elsewhere. The new technique used the Jews themselves as their own oppressors. How satisfying this must have been to the Master Race. So now, when the Germans needed workers of a certain skill, age, gender, etc., they instructed the Judenrat to collect and deliver them. The Judenrat, having a census of all the Jews, would make a list fulfilling the requirements, and the Militz would go out, pick up the people, and hand them over to the Nazis.

By early 1940 it wasn't unusual for 500 or more able bodied men and boys to be rounded up and taken to parts unknown. Those thus transported were usually told that they were going away for a few months, and then would be returned home. Of the thousands of Jews of all ages who were picked up and sent to labor camps from Bendzin, I know of only two boys who were ever sent back to Bendzin during the war's duration.* The boys reported that they had spent the entire time they were away working in a bomb factory on 12-hour a day shifts, seven days a week.

In the long run, those sent away early in the war probably had a better chance of survival than those who stayed in Bendzin. However, many of us went to extreme measures to avoid being torn from our families and sent away to an unknown fate. For example, when Moishe learned that he was on a list to be sent to a labor camp, he spread some caustic substance on his arm and wrapped it up. He soon had a horrible looking ulcerated sore, for which he concocted some reasonable story to explain how he got it. He reported for transportation as ordered, but one look at this "unfortunate injury," and they scratched him off the list and sent him home. He carried this scar with him to the grave, more than sixty years later.

The Nazis insisted that everyone old enough to work must work, preferably at something that would help the German war effort. Unemployment was tantamount to a ticket to a labor camp. Being employed, as it worked out, only postponed transportation—to a labor camp in the early days, or to a death camp later on.

*I have heard that there were others who returned, but personally only knew of two.

CHAPTER FIVE

Close Call for Moishe
(As told by Moishe)

One morning, I was watching as the SS brought a group of about fifty older Jewish men into the public square. Many were veterans of World War I. The men were divided into groups– over here were put those who fought on one side, over there those who fought on the other side, and in another place, those who didn't fight at all. An SS officer with a big beer belly was obviously in charge, as he continually shouted commands at his troops, and insults at the prisoners.

Walking over to those who had fought with the Germans in 1914, the fat officer sneered at them, and scoffed, "It was because of you Goddamned Jew dogs that we lost the war."

But then to the Jew who fought on the Russian side, the Nazi said something like, "Jewish dog, you killed my father."

To those who had served in the Polish army in 1939, the Nazi would say, while kicking the victim, "So, Jew dog, you want to kill me, do you?"

To those who had not fought at all, "You greedy Jew pig, while everyone else was in a foxhole, you were taking advantage of the war by getting rich on the black market."

All of the men were taunted and ordered to perform impossible tasks, such as jumping over huge obstacles, and when they inevitably failed, were brutally kicked and beaten.

A great many Poles were also abused and sent away for labor, but they weren't treated with the same level of contempt, degradation and brutality as the Jews, unless perhaps, they might be caught helping a Jew. Many Poles did assist the Nazis by pointing out Jews and by turning in Jews who were in hiding, but many also helped the Jews, even at the risk of their own lives. Those who helped the Nazis did so either in the hope that their actions would ingratiate them with the Nazis and thus make their lives safer or better, or they were happy to help the Nazis because they were staunch anti-Semites themselves. This latter group comprised a large sector of the Polish population. The Nazis benefited a great deal from the assistance of these people. From just the point of view of our being identified as Jewish, we had more to fear from these anti-Semitic Poles than from the Germans, for to the Germans we might just look like Poles, but the Poles could often tell that we were Jewish.

One of the early effects of the occupation was a sharp increase in the cost of purchasing new shoes. Our old sources were unreachable, and any new source was more expensive. The Nazis had demonstrated that raising prices was a capital offence, so we were forced to sell at little or no profit, or sometimes at a loss.

The first day we opened our door for business, the store was flooded with Poles wanting to buy shoes at bargain prices. Before lunchtime, every last shoe was gone. About six o'clock in the evening, two German soldiers marched into the store, but not before my father scooted out the back door. We didn't want the store to be left unattended and defenseless, so we had agreed that one of us should take off if we saw trouble coming. The soldiers wasted no time asking questions, but ordered me to go with them, and escorted me to the local army headquarters. But, thanks to his alertness, at least Father was still free.

The first thing I saw as we approached the headquarters was a group of elderly Orthodox Jews, on their hands and knees, scrubbing the sidewalk and steps in front of the building with their prayer shawls. German soldiers and a few Poles were standing around laughing at this humiliating spectacle, while the soldier overseeing them kept bellowing, "Schnell! Schnell! Schnell!" (Faster! Faster! Faster!), giving the audience cause to laugh ever harder.

This verified for me that I had not been invited for tea. I was directed into a room in which there were about a dozen Jewish men of various ages, including two elderly bakers whom I knew from the neighborhood. All of the men were standing rigidly with their arms raised above their heads. A brutish soldier was sitting on a chair in the corner, scowling at his sub-human charges. Of course, I was immediately ordered to put my hands up high and keep them there. Holding ones hands up becomes very painful after a few minutes, and before long it is almost unbearable, so one of the men could stand it no longer and dropped his arms. Immediately the guard shouted at him, "Get your hands back up!"

The menacing tone in the guard's voice left no doubt that he was to be strictly obeyed. I was in agony, and every second felt that I couldn't take another minute of this, but one glance at this vicious guard persuaded me that I had no choice but to bear the pain. I would never have believed how much suffering a person can endure when he has no options. Every time the door to the inner office would open, I and the others felt a glimmer of hope that maybe something was going to happen to end this ordeal, but our tormentors were in no hurry. Time crept slowly by as our arms went numb, and the pain in our shoulders got worse. I finally decided to try something—maybe if I bent down to tie my shoe, I might get away with it and garner a few precious seconds of relief. So, gritting my teeth, I slowly bent over and tied one shoelace, then put my arms back up. To my surprise, the soldier just gave me a dirty look, but said nothing. I began thinking—if he let me tie one shoe, maybe I could get away with tying the other shoe. After a few minutes, I let my arms down and bent over to tie the other shoe. In an instant, the soldier jumped to his feet and screamed at me, "You Goddamned Jew dog, put your hands back up and keep them there!" At least I had gotten my few seconds of relief from my pain, and I hadn't been struck with a rifle butt to pay for it.

Our torture continued unabated until about eight o'clock, when the door to the inner office opened, and we finally began to be summoned inside, one at a time. The rest of us were still compelled to keep our arms up. Each time the door swung open, I would pray, "Dear God, let it be my turn."

When I was eventually called into the inner office, my head was reeling from my hours of torment. My head was spinning so, I lost touch with my surroundings. By the time I recovered my senses, I found myself standing in front of a bare wooden table, be-hind which was seated a very grim looking German officer. There were also several soldiers in the room, on both sides and behind me. Beside the table stood a middle-aged Polish woman. The of-ficer glared at me, and sternly declared, "You have been accused by this woman of quoting her 12 złotys for a pair of shoes, when she had bought the same shoes before the war for 10 złotys. Why did you ask for more money for the shoes, when you know it is not permitted?"

I shook my head and respectfully answered, "No sir, I didn't do it."

The officer frowned and turned to the woman. "Is this the man who sold you the shoes?"

The woman took a long look at me and reluctantly said, "No, it's not."

When she said *this*, I could have kissed her, ugly as she was, and I said to myself, "Whew! I'm off the hook!"

Turning back to me, the German asked, "Who was in the store this morning, when she went in there?"

"That must have been my uncle. He is the owner. I don't usu-ally work there, but I was helping out this afternoon."

"Did he tell you to raise the prices?"

"No sir. He said to keep the same prices as before the war, but let me explain something. The shoes this lady looked at may have looked just like the ones she bought before, but maybe these were made of a better grade of leather and therefore cost a little more. The same style shoes are often made in more than one grade of leather."

The officer stared blankly at me as I was making this explana-tion, then with no change of expression simply said, "Go."

He might as well have said, "You won't be hanged today, after all."

I was escorted back to the waiting room, where I and a few others just sat until about eleven o'clock. A soldier came in and told us that we could go home, but to walk close to the wall, not in the middle of the street. Going outside, we were immediately blinded by the darkness; the moon was absent and due to the wartime blackout, there wasn't a glimmer of light in the entire city. Our group of about a half dozen survivors of the interrogations began groping our way anxiously homeward, as our eyes slowly adjusted to the dark. We had stumbled for only about a block before we were stunned by a bright light assaulting our eyes, followed by the shout, "Halt! Hands up!"

The German patrol approaching us demanded, "Where are you coming from? Why are you on the street at this hour?"

"We were being interrogated at the commandant's office, and they just now let us go home."

"How far do you have to go?"

We all pleaded that it was only a block or two.

"Well then, move along, but stay close to the wall. Don't be out in the middle of the street."

We wasted no time in accepting this invitation. Of course, when I got to our apartment building, the big outside doors were bolted shut. This was not good. I knocked on the door—no response– so I knocked, and knocked, and knocked, and knocked, but there was no response. So I knocked a little harder, but there was still no sound from inside. I was beginning to panic; if I banged too loudly, I might attract unwanted attention, but if I were stuck outside, another patrol was certain to come along, and might not be as considerate as the last one. I was picturing myself being hauled off in a truck to parts unknown. Sweating profusely in spite of the chill morning air, I *really* banged on the door. This time it finally worked, and the Polish woman, Juskowa, who managed the building, and lived right by the front doors, opened up and let me in. She let me know that she was less than happy to be aroused from her sleep to perform this little chore, but I was so glad to be safely off the street that I didn't care what she said.

Next morning, no sooner had we opened up the shoe store than we were told that we should close it again. There was no explanation; all the Jewish stores were closed. The Germans had been spreading the propaganda that they were going to take away all the Jewish stores, factories, diamonds, and whatever else we might possess, and give it to the Aryans. Juskowa, our apartment caretaker, was a Pole and Poles were Aryans (at least in her mind, whether in eyes of the Germans or not); therefore was she not one of the rightful heirs to some of that Jewish property? Seizing this once-in-a-lifetime opportunity, Juskowa, stood in front of the store, and when a German would pass by, she would greet him with smiles and laughter, and tell him that he should give the shoe store to her. Full of hope of attaining the economic status she rightly deserved, she reasoned that since the Germans were all-powerful, any soldier passing by could, and should, give her the store. After making her impassioned plea to a number soldiers and being totally ignored, she gave up and went home—shoulder-bent with disappointment, and still storeless.

Meanwhile, we had to face the real possibility of the imminent loss of the store and its inventory. I had to do something to save at least some of the inventory, so I came back alone that night, making sure that no one could observe my activity, I hastily tied up most of the shoes into small bundles, and put the bundles here and there in various hiding places.

As it turned out, our fears of losing the store permanently were justified, but just a little premature. We were allowed to reopen, but were constantly reminded that our only means of livelihood could be terminated at any time at the whim of the Nazis.

CHAPTER SIX

Yellow Stars and Lost Stores
(As told by Moishe)

The time had come for our family to take some bold actions. If we just drifted along hoping for the best, sooner or later we would have no stock of shoes and no way to make a living. This was a serious matter, and we had many heated arguments about it. Mother wanted to start hiding shoes immediately, but Father was scared, and with good reason, for if we were caught we would be severely punished, perhaps even hanged. Hanging was a favorite Nazi method to set an example. But Mother insisted that we had to take that chance. Father would not agree, picturing himself dangling in the market square like the baker. So, in violation of the German orders, when Father was not around, Mother and I would secretly smuggle home a few shoes as a cache to fall back on. Mr. Klajnman, our neighbor, made his living by cutting up large sheets of leather to make shoe tops. He stored his stock of hides in the attic. Mother and I hid the smuggled shoes under Mr. Klajnman's pile of leather, where no one, Germans, Melitz, or anyone else would be likely to find them. Since Father was the most likely to be questioned, we didn't tell him where they were, so he couldn't tell the Nazis, even under harsh interrogation. The decision to hide these shoes turned out to be another vital link in our chain of survival; later on, these shoes literally saved our lives. Without the money we made from them, many of the things we did to save ourselves would not have been possible. Although we benefited from many strokes of luck, some of that luck was derived from making fortunate decisions, such as this hiding of the shoes. We were living in constant fear, but this fear made us more alert and sharpened our instincts, so we would make wiser decisions.

On October 28, 1939 the Nazis issued the order that all Jews, except children, must wear a white armband with a blue Star of David on it. This system was short-lived, however, as it was too easy for a Jew simply to remove the armband to enter some forbidden area and just slip it back on before leaving. So on November 23, the armbands were replaced with a bright yellow Star of David sewn on both the front and the back of our outer garments.

By the end of October, we had sold virtually all the remaining shoes in the store from the stock we had managed to replenish. We were now thankful that Mother had won the earlier debate about whether or not to secrete away some of the shoes into the attic. Along with the debate over the shoes, was a discussion about how to preserve what cash we had. Father wanted to convert it into US dollars, whereas Mother wanted to buy as much gold coins as possible. She realized that gold would be valuable no matter what the political or military situation around us. Fortunately for us, Mother prevailed in this decision as well. Within a very short time US dollars would have been absolutely useless for us, whereas the gold we saved turned out to be a life saver.

We were not greatly surprised when one day in early November, a tall man in a business suit, whom we had never seen before this day, entered the door of the shoe store and announced, "You must close down the store and make an inventory of all your stock. From now on you are working for me." Our new boss man was a Volksdeutsch from Trzebin whose name was Theo Lalushna, and ours was just one of several stores which had been given to him. By this time we were almost out of merchandise anyway. The concerns at the start of the invasion about keeping prices constant had become almost a moot issue —as we had so few shoes to sell anyway. The secret cache of extra shoes stored in the attic remained intact, but we didn't want to tap into that cache, until it was absolutely necessary. So, as the situation was, we weren't much worse off when we were shut down and our store taken away from us, as were all other Jewish businesses. Although he was a complete stranger to us at this time, Theo was to play a huge part in our eventual survival. He kept Father and me on to run the store, paying us a small salary, and with his connections, he was able to keep a reasonable stock of shoes. Working for another man in what had been his own store was extremely hard on Father emotionally. One day he just collapsed in the store, and after that Mother wouldn't let him go back for several weeks. So I was left to run the store by myself. However, we were very lucky to have Theo as our boss. He treated us with respect, and most importantly he allowed us to use some of his valuable shoe purchasing coupons to buy shoes for ourselves, and then resell them on the black market to help feed our family.

The German genius for organization and total control was increasingly evident. In early 1940 the Germans expanded the Judenrat into what was called the Jewish Federation–under total German control of course. This was still essentially a collection of Jews put in "leadership" positions by the Germans. In the Bendzin area, the Jewish Federation was officially called the Union of Jewish Communities of Upper Silesia. The Germans appointed as its head Moniek Merin, the leader of the Bendzin Judenrat. The Germans required that Jews could only deal with the Jewish Federation–all purchases of food, clothing, or whatever, had to be made through the Federation. All Jews were given a very limited number of ration coupons, which had to be presented in order to buy anything. Naturally, this system quickly spawned a thriving and very lucrative black market for those selling coupons, and a very expensive market for the buyer. The opportunities for corruption among the Jewish "leaders" were clearly very great, and many yielded to the temptation. On a rare occasion, a top Judenrat administrator would see himself as some kind of Lord, and ride roughshod over his fiefdom. But it seems that Moniek Merin came to believe that he was called to an heroic mission to serve and save the Jewish people throughout Europe, and that he could use his "leadership" position to do so. Toward this end, he worked with great vigor and cunning to gain full control over all the Jewish councils in eastern Upper Silesia. In Bendzin, he hired and fired four Judenrat chairmen before he found one who would do his bidding without question. Because of the economic value of the area, from the beginning the Germans had put eastern Upper Silesia directly into the Reich. It was not part of the so-called General Government, or "protectorate," to the northeast, which took in virtually all the rest Poland. Merin was in charge of rounding up the workers for slave labor camps, which of course made him enormously unpopular with all the Jews. He instituted a system whereby a family could buy out their young person's service at the work camp, but he set the price at 15,000 złotys per laborer. What was worse, many families somehow raised and paid Merin this incredible amount of money—more than most people made in several years of work–only to have their son or daughter taken away by the Germans anyway.

In the early spring of 1941 all the Jews from the ghetto in the nearby town of Oswiencim, now renamed Auschwitz, were relocated to Bendzin, Sosnowiec and Chrzanow. These new residents of Bendzin reported that the Germans had been building a huge new prison camp at Oswiencim, on the site of a former Polish army cavalry camp. They didn't know why they were suddenly taken away from their ghetto and moved to Bendzin. Although no one was aware at the time, the Nazis were in the process of creating at Auschwitz the largest and most efficient *murder machine* in the history of mankind, and they didn't want any Jews to witness this process. Of course, most of them eventually were taken back "home", and gassed and cremated in the newly completed Auschwitz death factory, along with more than a million other Jews from across Europe who made the fatal one-way trip. Since Bendzin was one of the last cities to be ghettoized, many Jews from other ghettos escaped and sought refuge there. This influx, together with forced relocations increased Bendzin's Jewish population to around fifty thousand at its peak.

At least our family had something to be thankful for: we were still together and in our own home —with the exception of my brother Issa. The last we had heard from or about him was shortly after he fled to Russia.

CHAPTER SEVEN

Issa's Russian Odyssey
(As told by Issa)

In September of 1939 I was 23 years old, a little more than ten years older than my little sister Dora. As soon as the invasion started I expected to be impressed into the Polish army, and that was the last thing I wanted. So, along with some of my friends, I went into hiding outside of Bendzin, and didn't come back home until after the Germans had taken Bendzin. I hadn't been home very long before David, my cousin on Father's side, came from Sosnowiec to our home. He was very solemn and hardly said a word. He took me off to the side so the rest of the family couldn't overhear our conversation.

"I'm going to Russia tomorrow," he told me, "and when I tell you what just happened, you'll want to go with me. Yesterday I was just walking down the street when a squad of German soldiers grabbed me and my friend, and shoved us into the back of a truck. They drove around the city streets picking up any young Jew 'til they had 20 of us in the back of that truck. We figured they were going send us off to a labor camp, but they took us out to the forest, and split us up into two groups—ten over here and ten over there. They gave me a shovel and ordered me and the other nine guys in my group to dig ten graves. When we finished digging them, the other ten were ordered to lie down in those graves. The son of a bitch of a Nazi officer ordered his men to shoot those poor guys who were just lying there, in the holes we'd dug for them. We were ordered to watch while those German bastards murdered them—many of them were our close friends—and we couldn't do a damned thing but stand there and watch. Then we had to cover them up. I'm still shaking. God only knows why I'm not lying out there in the forest. They took down our names and addresses, then let us go, but they said that if they heard one word in town about what just happened, the same thing would happen to all of us."

David had good reason to be scared. The Germans had his name and address, and no doubt at least one of his fellow survivors would sooner or later open his mouth to someone. Escaping to Russia immediately seemed like a good idea, so he came to Bendzin hoping I would go with him. I was easily persuaded.

Mother sewed all the złotys she could scrape up into the lining of my coat, into my shoes, and pinned some in my underwear. The family gave me their blessing, and I left—we never said "goodbye" to each other when someone left. I got Israel Szyjowicz (the son of Joivele Szyjowicz the baker), a close friend of mine, to go with us, and the three of us hopped on a train bound for the city of Sanok, on the San River, which was the current German-Russian border. We hoped to reach the city of Lemberg* in the Soviet zone of Poland.

The three of us, along with a large number of other young Jews, got to Sanok without any problem, but how the Russians might welcome us if we made it across the river without being caught by the Germans, was something we would have to find out. Being complete strangers to the area, we were at a loss as to what to do next.

While we were pondering our problems, a Ukrainian man managed somehow to gain our confidence. He offered to take about ten of us, boys and girls, across the river early the next morning before the sun came up. All he asked for was a small fee, which wasn't really all that small. Not having any better idea of what to do, we naively agreed to put our trust in him, and gave him the money he asked for. This kind fellow obligingly let us spend the night in his house. Early in the morning we were jarred out of our sleep, not by the Ukrainian but by two German soldiers, who promptly arrested all of us and whisked us off to the nearest German army headquarters. My worst fear had come true. This duplicitous Ukrainian had done quite well for himself—made a nice profit and ingratiated himself with the Germans at the same time, and probably got some reward to boot. During this arrest process Israel and I were separated from David. I don't know what they did with him, but I never saw him again.

At headquarters, Israel and I were ordered to stand at attention in front of a no-nonsense German officer. The officer began his interrogation by ordering us to take off our pants. I tried to protest. I would have meekly complied, but for the fact that also in the room was a young woman, and I and my friend felt very embarrassed to strip in front of the girl. The officer, not in the mood to debate the issue, gave us two choices: we could obey his orders without question or be taken out and shot. Since he put it that way, we began to strip. The officer carefully searched our pants, and finding nothing of interest, tossed them aside, and ordered one of his men to do a thorough search.

Having foreseen the likelihood of being caught, Mother and I had "hidden" some money–about 40 złotys–in my underwear for any soldiers, guards, or authorities to find. I put on a good show of trying to avoid having my underwear frisked, twisting my body around and claiming that I had nothing worth finding. But the soldier wasn't fooled and quickly located the money in the underwear. My attempt to hide the money seemed to infuriate the soldier and he started beating me. This was actually a good sign as it meant that the search was over. But the fun was just beginning.

"What is your name?" the officer demanded.

I answered, "Isaac Szpringer."

For some reason, this infuriated the officer, who punched me so hard right in the face that I fell to the ground.

"What is your name?" the officer screamed again as I struggled to my feet.

"Isaac Szpringer."

This resulted in another punch to the face and a return trip to the ground.

Yet again, the officer demanded, "What is your name?"

I started to cry, "Look, if I say my name you just hit me, so I'm not going to say anything."

The officer screamed at me that Szpringer was a good German name, and that no stinking Jew should have a German name.

But this was still September, 1939, before the "final solution" had been initiated, so after a few more choice words, the officer told his men to take me and my friend to the Russian border, which at this time was the River San. So the soldiers marched Israel and me to the San. We could see Russian soldiers milling about on the other side of the river. "Swim," one of the Germans commanded, shooting his rifle in the air to emphasize his demand. Neither of us were good swimmers, but choosing the possibility of drowning over the certainty of being shot, we quickly jumped in, and to our surprise discovered the river was actually quite shallow and we could just wade across. Not having had enough fun yet, the German soldiers started shooting in the water around us and over our heads.

With a big laugh, the Russian soldiers pulled two soaking wet Jews out of the river and escorted us to the local army headquarters, in the city of Lemberg, which was where we wanted to go in the first place. After a short, but intense interrogation, the Russians decided that we were harmless, and having no use for two Jews at the moment, they let us go. Now that we were in Lemberg, we really had no great plan as to what to do next. Wandering around the city, Israel and I met a wealthy man who invited us to take a room in his house, a very large plush home. We didn't know why he as being so generous, but we weren't about to look a gift horse in the mouth. Later we figured out why he wanted us and others to live in his house—now that the Russians were in control of the city, he was afraid that they would take away his property if they saw how rich he was, so he wanted his home to look like a boarding house.

We had no other way to make a living, so Israel and I started trading on the black-market. We were dealing mostly in cigarettes and saccharine. Business was very good, and we soon had a fair pile of money. We decided that one of us should return to Bendzin and buy a stock of goods, which were much cheaper in Poland than in Russia. Israel's family was very poor, so we agreed that he should give half of the money he took back to his family and buy tradable goods with the rest. What we hadn't figured on was that the border was no longer so porous, and he couldn't get back to Lemberg. Since my family never saw any of the money, he obviously just pocketed my share.

Shortly after his return to Bendzin, Israel joined the Jewish police (Militz). He strutted around town in his neat, new Militz uniform – dark pants and shirt with no insignia, and a white cap with blue band and black bill. Mother noticed that he was obviously avoiding the Szpringers, so she confronted him, and asked him if he thought he was too good for them, now that he had a white hat on. He apologized to her – a dressing down by Mother could be rather humbling—but, of course, didn't tell her about the money. Israel was a tall, good looking young man, but buried under that handsome façade a devil lay dormant. He became one of the most treacherous and cruel of the Militz, all of whom were considered traitors by most of the other Jews. But despite his short time "on top" as a Melitz sergeant, Israel Szyjowicz met the same fate that befell most Polish Jews: he was eventually sent to Auschwitz. No doubt, he thought he would get preferential treatment there because of all the help he had given the Nazis, but a bunch of his fellow prisoners, from Bendzin, threw a bag over his head and beat him to death. He pleaded with one of them, whom he thought was a friend, to help him, but this fellow said, "Nobody can help you. You've caused the death of too many Jews."

The Russian authorities in Lemberg caught up with me and gave me a choice: go back to Poland or go east to a waiting job in a Russian coal mine. Going back to Poland wasn't something I wanted to do, but working in a coalmine didn't sound too enticing either. So I decided to just hide out until a better option came along. When my landlord discovered that I was hiding from the authorities, he threw me out, not wanting any trouble in his house. Out on my own, with nowhere to live, within days I was arrested by the Russians. As irony would have it, I was now accused of being a German spy. I wasn't offered any choices now; I was just put on a train and sent to the frigid forest of Finland, where I was set to work cutting down and hauling trees for the war effort.

I should have chosen to work in the coalmine when I had the chance. Already in late September deep snow covered everything and the temperatures, freezing in the daytime, were sub-zero at night.

We were given just enough food to keep us alive, and we were worked from sunup to sundown. Most of the prisoners weren't men who were used to hard physical labor, and the extreme conditions were too much for them. Many of them just got weaker by the day and soon died. I had never done hard work myself and had a very rough time in the beginning, but somehow was able to hang on until I became tough enough to keep up with the work and adjust to the harsh conditions.

While we were in Finland, Hitler broke his promise to Stalin (which I'm sure was no big surprise to anyone), and attacked Russia. With the German forces closing in on us, the Russians abandoned the camp. We were herded into a ship, where we spent forty days and forty nights below decks before arriving at our new camp in Siberia. Perhaps it wasn't quite that long, but it seemed like it.

Conditions in the new camp were even harsher than in Finland, but by this time those of us who had survived were better adjusted to living on the edge of survival. However, men continued to succumb to the unrelenting hardships. When we came back from work each day, we got a piece of bread and a little soup. If the overseer said we did a good job we got 700 grams of bread, but if he said we didn't do a good job we got 300 grams of bread. As a result the strong stayed strong and the weak got weaker.

In the long run, the majority of the prisoners died from being over-worked and under-fed. The only crime most of these pathetic fellows were guilty of was trying to save their skins by escaping from the Germans by going to Russia. When they died, their bodies were unceremoniously tossed into a pit and covered with a thin layer of dirt. The wolves appreciated this skimpy burial. At night we could hear them gnawing on the bones of the corpses. The wolves were better fed than we were.

The camp had a doctor, whose entire medical facility was one small house with one perpetually empty bed. One day I felt so sick that I didn't think I could make it through the day, so I went to the doctor, who stuck an ice-cold thermometer into my mouth and retrieved it in a few seconds, declaring that I didn't have any fever, so I was sent back out to work. Apparently the camp policy was that by definition, no one was ever sick, of course the prisoners and the wolves knew better.

This life went on day after weary day, with no rest for weekends, holidays, or anything else. Every day was the same: waking up in darkness, cutting down trees with a long two-man saw, hauling the resulting logs away all day, and going to bed hungry, hoping to recover enough strength to make it through the next day. The guards at the camp were either very old soldiers–too old for fighting at the front, which in the 40's in Russia, meant very old and broken down indeed—or they had been wounded in battle and were only fit enough for such duty as guarding prisoners. Life for the guards was also harsh, but at least they were better fed and clothed than their charges.

Still, there was no doubt about who was in charge, that is, who had the guns and the power. Being a very religious Orthodox Jew, it bothered my conscience to work on an important Jewish holiday, so in my first year in the Siberian camp, when Rosh Hashanah came around I decided to take the day off. The soldier in charge of my work detail discovered that I was not at work, and went back to my barrack to find me lying on my bunk. Poking me with his rifle, he demanded to know, "Why the Hell aren't you working?" I told him that I was sick, and the doctor had told me to stay in my bunk for the day. This old soldier had been around long enough to know a goldbricker when he saw one, especially since he knew that the doctor never excused anyone from work. Pushing me at bayonet point out to where my crew was working, he ordered me to stand there in the icy wind for the rest of the day, not letting me work to keep warm. I got my day off from work, but not what I had in mind. Not surprisingly, I didn't try to avoid working on religious holidays after that.

In early 1943 many of us got a welcome surprise. The Russians finally realized that they were wasting a lot of skilled manpower cutting down trees, so they selected those of us who could do something more useful for the war effort and sent us to various places. The tailors were sent to garment factories; the barbers were sent to barber shops, and since I had listed my occupation as a shoemaker, even though I never was a shoemaker, I was sent to a shoe factory in the city of Solikamsk. I was still not a free man, but it was a huge improvement over the labor camp.

On my first day of work I saw a man across the room standing with a broom. I recognized him as a Jewish man we used to buy shoes from in Krakow. He was a millionaire who owned a shoe factory and was one of the richest men in the city, and here he was, sweeping the floor with a broom. I called over to him, "Mr. Ziperstein."

He came closer to me and said to me very sternly, "Don't call me Mister. My name is Ziperstein, call me Ziperstein."

It should have occurred to me that as a prisoner in communist Russia, the last thing he would want, was to be discovered as a capitalist millionaire.

One day, after several months working in the shoe factory, they told me to leave—I was a free man. I asked them where I should go to get work, but they just told me I was free and on my own.

I wandered around asking people where I might find a job. Someone suggested that I might find work at the train station. This sounded reasonable to me, for the railways must certainly be very busy transporting men and materiel for the war effort, so I walked to the station and approached the stationmaster. The stationmaster gave me a piece of paper permitting me one meal at the station kitchen, and told me to come back to him after I had eaten my fill. I returned at once to the station master, happy, well fed, and ready to do whatever my benefactor wished. He told me to go to the orchard and see that nobody stole the fruit, and come back at twelve o'clock. So I went to the orchard, where I had nothing to do but watch the trees. It was very warm and quiet, so I sat down against a tree and immediately fell asleep. When I didn't show up at noon, the manager sent a girl to look for me, but she couldn't find me anywhere, so she went back to the station. The manager couldn't imagine what had become of me, so he sent out several girls to find me, which they did, fast asleep against the tree. When the manager heard that I was sleeping on the job he was thoroughly disgusted. He told me, "I gave you such a nice, easy job just watching our trees, and you couldn't even do that. Get out of here. You're fired!"

I begged him to reconsider, but it did no good, so I was back on the street. Another person suggested that I might get work at the bakery, which I did.

The first job I was given was as a water carrier, which greatly pleased the girls working there, especially since I was the only man around. The manager of my area of the bakery was a Jewish girl named Eda Davidonau. The mayor of the city was also Jewish. But I thought it best to pretend to be a Pole rather than a Jew. Later on, I was assigned to a job in another place, but I didn't want to leave Eda, with whom I had become infatuated, and thought she felt the same way. So I went to her in secret and confessed that I was Jewish, not Polish. Eda then confessed to me that she was very happy I told her this, because all of her family had been killed in Poland in a pogrom, and she had been secretly planning to murder me because she thought I was a Pole. So instead of killing me, she gave me a new job as the assistant manager.

I stayed on in Solikamsk until the end of the war. Eda and I had developed a loving relationship and I wanted her to go back with me to Bendzin. She said she would be happy to go with me anywhere—anywhere that is, except Poland. All of my pleading and cajoling didn't make a dent in her resolve; she hated the Poles and would not set foot in Poland. It broke my heart to leave her, but I urgently wanted to get back to my family as soon as possible. Reluctantly saying goodbye to my beloved Eda, I struck out, and headed west. I still could not believe even half of the horrible rumors that I had been hearing about what the Germans had done to the Jews.

I got as far as the Ukraine, where I ran into the brick wall of Russian bureaucracy. They were not issuing any exit permits to anyone, as far as I could tell. So while I cooled my heels waiting to get into Poland, I began buying and selling various merchandise, on the black market of course, and actually made enough money to put a few rubles in my pocket.

*This Polish city, as of 1340, was called L'wow. It became Lemberg, as part of the Austrian Empire 1772 to 1919, when it went back to Poland. When the Germans and the Russians divided Poland in 1939 L'wow fell into the Soviet sphere. It is now in Ukraine, and called L'viv or L'vov.

CHAPTER EIGHT

A Miracle at the Sports Stadium
(Told by Dora)

Meanwhile, far from Russia, the three years between my brother
Issa's leaving us in September of 1939 and the summer of 1942 our
lives in Bendzin became more deprived and threatened with each
passing day. Our neighbors continued to be rounded up, and to
disappear. In May of 1942 the first large-scale mass transportation
from Bendzin took place, with 2000 Jews being sent to Auschwitz,
which had been developed into a mass murder machine just about
two months earlier. To accelerate the rate of homicides, the Nazis
built a much larger death camp nearby, called Auschwitz II or
Birkenau, which started operation on June 30, 1942.

Any hope that our condition might improve was dramatically
dashed on August 12, 1942. A few days prior, the Germans gave
orders that at 5 a.m. on that day all Jews must report to either the
Sarmacia sport stadium, or the Hakoach sport stadium, supposedly to receive some new stamp on our ID papers. We were told
to go there dressed in our finest clothes—both men and women.
Anyone not obeying these orders would be deported to the east
and their possessions confiscated. We were all terrified and confused. Should we obey this order or hide? Almost everyone came
to realize that our only realistic option was to obey the order. The
only exceptions were some members of the youth groups, who
were more defiant than the rest of us. One thing that was ominous about this order was that all the major towns in the area were
given this command on the same date. About week earlier, in an
attempt to trick us into complacency, the Nazis had made the same
demand to the small town of Cheladz about three kilometers from
Bendzin, and had detained only a few unemployed youths, and

had sent the rest of the people home with newly stamped papers. This maneuver didn't calm the fears of too many people, even though the Judenrat was urging everyone to comply, saying that we had nothing to worry about. Some of the factory owners told their workers that as long as they were doing work that was helpful to the Germans, they needn't worry. This made some sense, but our experience had shown that when it came to the Jews, economic interest didn't seem to guide the actions of the Gestapo or the SS.

So, before 5 a.m., on August 12, our whole family, except of course Issa, who we hoped was in Russia, got up and walked to an assembly point, as ordered, as did the vast majority of Bendzin's Jews. From this point we were marched to the Sarmacia stadium. As we approached the stadium, we were greeted by the sight of soldiers with machine guns stationed in the fields around the stadium. Many other soldiers on horseback, or on foot with dogs on taut leashes, patrolled around the outside. Masses of people of all ages streamed through the gate into the field inside—elderly parents and grandparents being held up by the younger family members, infirm folks being pushed in wheelchairs, women pushing baby carriages, mothers with infants in their arms, and small children clinging fast to their parents or older sibling's hands.

Many of us were seized by a sickening realization that we should probably not have come, but it was too late to do anything but follow the crowd and obey orders. Inside the scene was as foreboding as that outside, with Gestapo and Jewish Militz herding the arriving mass into an area on one side of the football field. Opposite us, on the other side, we could see that a mixture of Militz and German guards had cordoned off three distinct areas. We didn't know what devilment they had planned, but we were soon to find out.

In the center of the field, in an ominous black uniform and brandishing a leather whip in his hand, a notoriously vicious SS officer named Mesinger* stood behind a small table. Anyone who had dealt with this Mesinger knew that no mercy of any kind should be expected. We were kept agonizing in the withering sun all morning long, having no clue about our fate, when finally, about one o'clock the Melitz began gathering up family groups and herding them up to face the menacing Mesinger. As each family group would stand before the table, Mesinger would just point his finger at each person and say ein or zwei, or drei—one or two, or three—indicating to which cordoned off area that person should go. Many people came up to the table waving their precious working papers, thinking that being employed would immunize them from being sent away, but Mesinger just ignored the papers and played God on his own terms–ein, zwei, drei. In the beginning, many people pleaded to not be separated from their families, but these people were severely beaten with truncheons and whips, and roughly driven to the group that Mesinger had selected for them. After witnessing this brutality, the rest of us got the message and the victims ceased to protest.

While avoiding being near the front of the mass of our fellow Jews for as long as we could, my parents and brothers were able to see a pattern in the distribution to the three groups. What they observed was, that whenever a large family approached the selection table, they were invariably broken up, and sent to two or more different groups. More significantly, they could see that the elderly, the sick, and the very young children were mostly being sent to Group Three; which almost certainly meant they were to be sent to Auschwitz. Able-bodied people were often sent to Group Two, and would most likely be sent to a slave labor camp. The rest ended up in Group One. We didn't know what was planned for Group One, but there was a chance that they might be spared for now. My elders were frantically struggling to come up with any plan that might improve our chances of not being separated. They reasoned that we could reduce the size of our family group we might stand a slightly better chance to avoid being split up. We were particularly worried about Laya, who was too young to even wear a yellow star, and would almost certainly be sent to Group Three. They must find a way to get Laya to Group One—and fast. Of course, ours wasn't the only family with realistic fears for their smaller children. Some of these families, when they thought they saw that the guards were looking the other way, would send their children racing to Group One. The families were helped in this attempt to save the children, by members of the youth groups, who bravely risked their own lives in doing so. Luckily, many of these children made it, but many were shot dead by the German guards as they fled. It's impossible to imagine the horror the parents felt as they helplessly watched as their child was killed like some game animal being shot for sport. They probably never forgave themselves for the fatal decision they had made, but these children were almost certainly doomed, no matter what they did.

My parents were not willing to have Laya take this risk. They hoped that there was a slight chance they might get some help from Israel Szyjowicz, since he used to be my brother Issa's closest friend, even though he was now known to be one of the more brutal of the Militz. So Yossel went over to Israel, and asked him if there was some way he could help them to save Laya.

Israel's sarcastic response was, "What do you want me to do, put her in my pocket? I have a little sister of my own, and I don't even know how to save her."

With no chance of help from Israel, and with time running short, Yossel knew he would have to find some way himself to give Laya any chance to avoid transportation to Auschwitz. Grabbing Laya by the arm, he took her over to a spot near the table, on the side nearest to Group One.

In a low, but very firm voice, he told her, "Don't ask any questions. Just do as I say. When you see a couple who are chosen to go to Group One, as soon as they head that way, run up and join them. Maybe the Germans will be too busy to notice you." Which was made more likely by the pandemonium that had taken over when the people figured out what was happening, and the police had their hands full controlling the panicking crowd. Some were so gripped with panic that they tried to run or climb out of the stadium, which, of course, meant instant death.

Yossel went right back to the family, leaving little Laya in a state of confusion, shaking with fear, but trusting her brother and looking for her chance to do what Yossel had told her to do. Amazingly, Yossel's quick thinking and bold action worked, and as a result Laya avoided an almost certain selection for death; but this was just the beginning of a series of narrow escapes on her part.

Laya appeared to be relatively safe for now, but the rest of us were still in great jeopardy. As more and more of the families became aware of what had happened to those families who had gone up to the table, there was a growing tendency for them to hold back. The Militz was having increasing difficulty in moving people up to the table. By this time, our family was in the forefront of the crowd, and seeing no possible way to avoid the inevitable, my father said to us, "We might as well go ahead and take our chances. We will put ourselves in the hands of God".

Resigning ourselves to Fate, the five of us—Father, Mother, Yossel, Moishe, and I—walked up together to face Mesinger, the self appointed God of Life and Death. Showing no more emotion than if he were selecting a new pair of pants, he waved his hand across all five of us and said, "Ein."

We were almost frozen in shock by this totally unprecedented decision, but maintained enough presence of mind to hurry over to Group One, where our first efforts were to find Laya. Searching through the crowd, we soon found her, crouching by the fence, trying to be as inconspicuous as possible. She had been cowering there, trying not to cry, all alone in wretched fear, for what must have seemed like forever to her. Having made it into Group One, united as a family again, we felt that we had a good chance to be sent home, but couldn't really be sure until the whole selection process was finished, and we were lined up to have our papers stamped. Watching the rest of the selection, we observed that after our *miraculous* escape from being separated, Mesinger gave no other family such a break—every other family, of the thousands that passed before him that dreadful day, were permanently broken up by Mesinger's fatal index finger—Ein, Zwei, Drei.

Why were we spared? We will never know, but I can think of two possible explanations: One, that when he saw that the people were drawing back, and showing resistance to being moved up to the table, he used us as an example to show the others that there was some chance for a whole family to be spared.

Another possibility is that Mesinger, by showing mercy to one family, could prove in his own mind, either consciously or subconsciously, that he had the power of God to spare a family, not just the power of the Devil to murder.

It was late at night by the time our papers were stamped, and we were allowed to go home. All the way home, we heard the piteous wailing and crying of those whose loved ones had been taken away that day, and that was every family except ours. The significance of the miracle we had received was not lost on us. We couldn't explain it, and we certainly did not take our good luck for granted. When we arrive at our front door, Mother drew us all close to her and said,

"I don't know why, but we have received a great blessing, and we must thank Him who has given it to us. I want every one of us to get down on our knees and kiss every step on the way up to our home."

We all knew how right Mother was, and one by one we tearfully kissed every single step as we climbed the stairs. There was very little talking in our home that night.

There is no question that escaping the selection with our whole family intact was our most significant stroke of luck, or perhaps miracle of the entire war. What was far more likely would have been for Father, Mother and probably Laya to have been selected for Group Three, and of course sent on to Auschwitz. It is also remarkable that neither Moishe, Yossel, nor I were sent to a slave labor camp that day via Group Two. Aside from smuggling Laya past the Nazis into Group One, we didn't really do anything that brought about our incredible luck. But perhaps, just that act of removing a child from our family group had made a difference.

For the next several days Bendzin was a city of tears. Mostly people just stayed in their homes mourning and praying. I would say that, at the most, only about one fourth of the people from our apartment complex returned to their homes the night of this devastating selection. The rest were on their way to Auschwitz or a slave labor camp. We felt very awkward about facing other families; how could we tell someone who had just lost a mother, a father, a child, or maybe all three, that we were all still together?

On a rise beside the railroad tracks sat four story building called the Sierociniec, which housed the orphanage until the War came to Bendzin. We in Bendzin were very proud of our orphanage, which had for many years been a kind refuge of mercy, but it became an anti-chamber to Hell in the hands of the Nazis. Prisoners awaiting transport to Auschwitz or labor camps were crammed into this building until being herded into cattle cars for a fateful journey. This selection was so large that the Nazis either could not arrange enough trains to ship everyone or they were not prepared to handle them at the receiving end. As a result, some Jews were sent home the next day, to the amazement and great joy of their families. This was indeed remarkable, as the Germans had such a well earned reputation for efficiency.

*Mesinger was in charge at the Sarmacia stadium and an SS officer named Kutchinski did the selection at the Hakoach stadium. After the war, several young survivors from Bendzin found out that one of these SS men was being held by the Soviets in a nearby prison. They went to the prison and told the Russian commandant that this man was responsible for the deaths of thousand including many of their own families. The commandant told them that he could do nothing about their claim, but that he could leave them in the cell with this Nazi, and if he happened to fall out of the third story window, it would be an accident as far as he was concerned. These young Jewish men considered this tempting proposition, but couldn't bring themselves to take their revenge into their own hands, so they walked away, hoping that somehow just would be done.

CHAPTER NINE

They Come for Me
(Told by Dora)

Following the selection at the Sarmacia and Hakoach sports stadiums, the deportation of Bendzin's Jews to Auschwitz and to slave labor camps continued, usually in smaller numbers, but sometimes as many as 2000 at a time.

One morning, in the fall of 1942, we were startled by a loud knocking on the door and the chilling demand: "Police! Open up!"

Having gotten the word, through the grapevine, that my name was on a roundup list, we knew they would soon be coming for me, but even before we had learned that I was wanted, the family had been making plans for hiding. In the bedroom where my parents slept was a large vertical standing stove, covered with ceramic tiles. My clever brother Yossel had removed the guts of the stove and cleaned it out to make a space for me or Laya to hide if necessary.

The Militz continued knocking on the door, but had to wait, since the door was made of steel, and they couldn't break it down even if they had wanted to. This delay was part of our plan.

Without a moment to lose, I quickly climbed inside the stove from the top, and when Yossel had replaced the top, I was standing in total blackness. Then came a clunk, as Yossel set a flower pot over my head as a final touch to my refuge. Yossel opened the front door and I could hear the boots of the Melitz pounding up the stairs, and into the kitchen.

"We have orders to pick up Dora Szpringer, where is she?" the sergeant in charge demanded.

Firmly and coolly, Mother told him, "She's not here. She's at her aunt's house." The sergeant immediately ordered his men to conduct a search of our home.

I was shaking with fear and tears were running down my cheeks, but I kept telling myself that I had to be strong; if I made the slightest sound, not only I but my whole family could face severe punishment—even transportation to Auschwitz. The noise of closet and cabinet doors being yanked open and slammed shut penetrated into my tiled cocoon, as the police searched every corner of our home. When the sound of their creaking footsteps passed by the stove, my heart was thumping so hard that I actually feared they might hear it. I expected any second to hear the lid pulled off and to see the face of a Melitz glowering down at me.

For some reason, to my immense relief, they missed the stove in their fruitless search, so the sergeant took his squad and left, but not without warning us, "We'll be back tomorrow, and she had better be here then."

Shaking and sweating, I was finally pulled out from my sooty sanctuary.

It would be a gross understatement to say that this had been an unpleasant experience for me, and one I wasn't looking forward to repeating. However, my fears were realized the very next day when, as promised, the Melitz returned. The same pounding on the door followed by the same demand as the day before: "Police! Open up!"

Back into the stove I went. But this time the sergeant didn't waste time making a search when I wasn't produced, but simply gave us the stern warning, "I'll be back tomorrow, and if Dora isn't here, we'll take you (my mother) in her place."

I don't know why we decided to ignore this warning; perhaps we thought that I might get lost in the tangle of orders the Militz had to carry out. Anyhow, forget me they didn't, but came back the next day as promised. Again I hid in the stove, and true to their threat, they took Mother away.

The next day, with the help of somebody, I don't know who, Father traced Mother to the Sierociniec. This former orphanage sat on a rise next to the railroad tracks, and was used by the Germans to hold the people who were rounded up, until they could be crammed into cattle cars trains bound for Auschwitz. Father also learned that Mother had given her captors a lot of trouble, which didn't surprise us too much, and for this they had severely beaten her with a table leg.

When Father returned home with this terrible news, both Laya and I were willing to turn ourselves in to ransom Mother. There was actually some serious consideration of letting Laya go in my place, for although I was older, I had never been a healthy child and Laya was stronger and more fit to handle hard labor. But, after much thoughtful discussion, it was decided that I should go. Had we been caught in any deception we all might have been transported to Auschwitz. My family tried to assure me that the Nazis would not have made such a fuss about picking me up if they just wanted to kill me; they must need me for some sort of work—in other words, slave labor. So I packed my little suitcase with a coat, a dress, a pair of shoes, and a few personal items, and set off on my lonely walk to the Sierociniec. I wasn't so much afraid of being killed as I was terrified of being separated from my family. I was scared and miserable, but loving my mother as I did, I felt no hesitation in taking this walk into the gates of Hell. Of course I wasn't even sure that they would let Mother go after I made my sacrifice.*

Unfortunately (or maybe fortunately), I remember very little of what happened to me in the orphanage or on the train to Auschwitz. As soon as I entered the building, I became a zombie. The reality of my situation was just more than I could face if I had to think about it, so I just withdrew into myself, became completely passive, and followed orders.

Since at this point I was separated from the rest of the family, I'll continue the relating of my individual experiences later in this narrative.

---

*The taking of my mother in my place, and her being beaten, was so traumatic to me that I completely blocked it from my memory for more than fifty years. When telling this story to my husband, or anyone, I said, and I believed it, that I turned myself in after they threatened to take Mother if I didn't show up. My sister was dumbfounded when she learned that I was telling the story this way. When she reminded me of what really happened, I broke down and cried uncontrollably, but I finally faced the awful truth. I suspect that there are still more Hellish realities hidden in some locked chamber of my mind.

CHAPTER TEN

From Home to Ghetto
(As told by Moishe)

In June, 1941, about a year and half before my sister Dora was taken from our family, the Germans double-crossed the Russians, attacking their old enemy with a massive, full scale invasion. The Russians may have been mentally prepared—they couldn't have overlooked the gathering of the German army on their border— but militarily they were far from being prepared, so they rapidly retreated, burning everything behind them. Not at all surprised by this German treachery, Mother just shook her head and said, as she often had, "You can't make a new friend out of an old enemy."

Common sense might lead you to reason that the invasion of Russia would be good news for the Jews of Poland. After all, the Germans had only a finite amount of resources and manpower, and would need it all to fight the Russians. Unfortunately for us, Hitler and his anti-Semitic henchmen didn't operate by common sense; they were on a crusade, and the murder of the Jews was given priority over the needs of their army. Although the Wehrmacht generals complained bitterly, valuable resources of transportation and manpower were siphoned off to the death camps for the rest of the war. For the Hitlerian gang, going into Russia provided their heinous crusade with another valuable resource—millions of more Jews to murder.

Under Theo's relatively benevolent control, we had been able to acquire quite a few new shoes to either squirrel away in the attic, or to sell on the black market, but in January, 1943, our fortunes took a turn for the worse. One day a taxi pulled up in front of the store, and a civilian whom we had never seen stepped out, accompanied by an SS officer. Striding into the store, the officer

commanded that we close the store immediately. Grabbing my father by the arm, he shoved him out the door, giving him a kick in
the back for good measure, and shouted at him to not come back.
The authorities had decided to split up Theo's little empire and
give some of his many stores to other Volksdeutsch. A Romanian
of German descent by the name of Josef Jarosz arrived in Bendzin,
and was awarded the right to take over our store. Jarosz was from
the Bessarabian part of Romania, where there were a great many
Germans, and their common language was German. The Soviets
had taken over and kicked out the Germans, sending them to
Germany.

Theo Lalushna tried very hard to keep our store, even offering
Jarosz two other stores instead. Theo thought he had made him a
generous offer, but the Romanian knew a good thing when he saw
it and refused him. One thing that Jarosz liked about our store was
that it had a back room, where he had plans to put in a shoe repair
shop. So our main source of income took a drastic hit as we came
under the control of this totally unsympathetic newcomer.

Josef Jarosz had no interest whatsoever in helping any Jews, but
he did keep me on to work in the store, simply because I actually
knew the business and Jarosz didn't. There was no Szpringer family shoe shop any more, and there never would be again. Jarosz
and his family were dyed-in-the-wool anti-Semites, and treated me
and any other Jew very harshly. As an example:

One day in early February, 1943, I saw the German flag flying
at half-mast, with a black banner on the flagstaff. Having virtually
no source of information about happenings in the world outside
of Bendzin, I didn't know what this meant. So I asked around, and
was told that this was a symbol of mourning by the Germans for
their crushing defeat at Stalingrad. Like most of the Jews, I didn't
even know there had been a battle at Stalingrad. But Germans
and their sympathizers were walking around with their heads
downcast, visibly shaken by the devastating defeat and loss of men
at Stalingrad. Jarosz told me, "We may lose the war, but before we
do, you'll be in the oven."

To reflect the feelings of her family, Josef Jarosz's 13-year-old
daughter walked over to me, called me, "You goddamned f—g

Jew", and gave me a swift kick in the shin, and of course, there was nothing I could do about it, except suffer the pain in silence.

We continued to sell our remaining contraband shoes on the black market to Poles who were only too happy to take them for far less than market value. And I continued to draw a meager salary from Jarosz. Any source of money was better than no money at all.

From early in the occupation, the Jewish section of Bendzin began to be ghettoized; that is, although there were no fences or walls sealing it off, we weren't permitted to live, or even walk, outside the area defined by designated streets. Of course, we were permitted to pass though the restricted zone on our way to and from work. As time went on, the area in which Jews were allowed to live was progressively reduced. People were given only a few days notice to gather their belongings and move out. They weren't told anything about where they could move to– just move out. We were fortunate that we were not located in the first areas of forced evacuations, but our part of town soon became very over-crowded. Many families were obliged to allow total strangers to move in with them.

When our cousin, Issa Felsensztien, his wife Bella, and their four year old daughter Chana, were forced out of their home, we gladly opened our home to them. Issa was a man in his late twenties, skinny, dark complexioned, with a low key personality. Bella was chunky but quite attractive and vivacious. Her major focus was a deep and total concern about the welfare of little Chana. The mother's good looks were amplified in her daughter, who was an exceptionally beautiful child. Her large, dark, serious eyes made you feel that she was much older and wiser than she really was. Having once seen this exceptional child, her face would be imprinted in your mind forever.

In January of '43, notices were posted around the city ordering that all Jews had just three days to evacuate Bendzin proper, and relocate in the area called the Kamionka, a rural area between Bendzin and Dambrowa. The Kamionka would now be the "Bendzin Ghetto." Agents of the Judenrat had the task of assigning living space to all the Jews forced to move to Kamionka. Of course, housing in this rural locale was woefully inadequate for all of the displaced people. Many families were simply assigned an open plot of land, where they fashioned a makeshift "home" by stretching sheets, or whatever they could scrounge, over furniture and poles. This provided them with a little privacy and some minimal protection from the weather.

Fortunately, Father managed to get us assigned to an empty stable that stood behind a two-story house.

The stable was divided into two parts: one side for cows and the other side for horses. Father took the horse side for our family because it was taller and had a hayloft overhead. Cousin Issa and his family moved into the cow side.

Both of our families needed to move as many of our valuable possessions as we could fit into the stable from our house in town to Kamionka, and there was little time. Only a small part of our possessions would fit into the little stable, and anything we couldn't move would be lost forever, so we selected only those things that we considered to be essential. Among the pieces brought to our new "home", were the two wardrobes, a bed, a couple of chairs, a small table, a nightstand, and a tub for water. In the short time we had, we did manage to sell some of the things we couldn't take with us to Poles for a fraction of their real worth. The big problem was how to carry what we needed to move, for a mile or more, out to the Kamionka. With his usual gumption, Yossel managed to get hold of an old wagon, and since we weren't able find a horse, we scrounged up some scraps of rope to make a sort of harness, and Yossel, Father, Cousin Issa, and I became horses. No one in our family was really used to hard manual labor, but we all leaned into our harnesses and pulled that old wagon full of goods and furniture all the way to the Kamionka, twice.

Everyone pitched in to clean up and fix up the stable; especially Yossel, who was a plasterer and jack-of-all-trades. He put in a wooden floor over the plain dirt of the barn, and plastered some of the walls. The place now looked more like a living space for people, rather than for horses. We also put in an oven, both for heat and for cooking. Our quarters began to take on a look of permanence, but we were well aware that the Germans had other plans for us; it was just a matter of when. To get water we had to go to the community well, which was across the road from the big house in front of the stable. We carried it in two buckets, hung from a yoke around the neck. This task usually fell, literally, on the shoulders of little Laya.

All Jews were confined to the Ghetto day and night, unless they had a permit to work in town. There was no fence around the Ghetto, so actually the border was quite porous for anyone bold enough to sneak out, but, of course, getting caught was a death sentence. Many brave young men slipped away to join guerillas hiding in the forest, known as partisans. Some of Yossel's and my friends tried to persuade us to go with them and join the partisans. The possible opportunity to fight back against these murderous Nazi beasts was definitely a great temptation, but we refused to follow this temptation, because we felt a strong obligation to stay with, and protect our family. If we had attempted to join the partisans, it was far from certain that we would have been successful, as many partisan groups were made up of Poles who didn't want any Jews in their group, and those who would take them in required any new members to come equipped with weapons, which we had no way of obtaining. Also, it often happened that some unscrupulous Poles would trick Jews into thinking they were being led to join the partisans, but would instead betray them to the Germans, for their own profit.

By the time our family moved to the Ghetto, Jarosz felt he knew the shoe business well enough to run the store without me, so he fired me. But I wanted and needed to work, so I was given a job with a crew cleaning up the houses that had been abandoned in town. One time as I was passing what was now the Jarosz shoe store, on an impulse, I quickly stepped into the store. I was taking a big risk because I wasn't supposed to leave my work for even a minute, but I was hungry and thought the Jaroszes might give me a bite of something to eat, considering all I had done for them. At first the wife was willing to let me have a piece of bread, but Jarosz himself refused to let me have anything. The wife, being a little more imaginative and shrewd than her husband, asked me, "Do you have any diamonds or gold you want to sell?"

"No, I don't have anything."

"How can that be? Everybody knows that Jews all have gold and diamonds."

"I don't have any gold or any diamonds."

"If you've got nothing to sell, we've got nothing for you."

So I went away hungry and feeling bit foolish for expecting to get anything from people like these.

After a few days I luckily found a job at the place where Yossel was already working—one of the factories making goods for the Germans, which was owned by a German by the name of Alfred Rossner. My job was to cut off the tops of old shoes and then fasten them to wooden soles for distribution to the slave labor camps. There was no shortage of material for this job, for in 1943 Auschwitz was producing a huge supply of shoes every single day. Yossel was a carpenter and plasterer at the Rossner plant. He was highly valued and was free to move about the factory.

Alfred Rossner courageously did all that was in his power to help the Jews to survive. For his efforts he was later murdered by the Nazis, and was to become honored as one of the "Righteous Among the Nations" in Israel after the war.

CHAPTER ELEVEN

A Place to Hide
(As told by Moishe)

As soon as the Germans began to round up and transport large groups of people from the Ghetto, all of the remaining Jews realized that their days were numbered. What could one do to avoid the next transport? With the exception of a few young men, who attempted to join the partisans, escape into the outside world had no meaning, as there was nowhere safe to go. Many naïve souls simply put their lives in the hands of the Almighty, and prayed for protection. Although everyone prayed, most people attempted to devise a more pragmatic plan, such as digging a hole and covering themselves, or running into and hiding in the nearby cornfield. If you could hide long enough, survival might be a possibility. Unfortunately, whether they attempted to hide or relied on Divine intervention, only a very few of Bendzin's Jews would see summer's end.

From the beginning, our family and Cousin Issa's family (the Felsensztiens) were much more fortunate than many of our fellow Ghetto dwellers, living in a building of our own, with a solid roof over our heads, but we knew that we were living on borrowed time. From the day that we settled into the Ghetto, all of us realized that the time for some sort of positive action was at hand, and time was of the essence. Our being spared at the selection at the Sarmacia stadium was a great miracle not likely to be repeated; Father, Mother and Laya all stood a good chance of being picked up and sent straight to the gas chambers of Auschwitz at any time, and Yossel and I were good candidates for slave labor.

A few months earlier, Father had gone over to Sosnowiec to visit his sister. While he was there, my aunt had shown him how their family had prepared a hiding place in the attic for what they considered the inevitable—the Nazis coming to take them away, sooner or later. My father quickly recognized that the stable had potential. It seemed quite possible to devise a hiding place in the hayloft where both families in the stable could scurry to in time of danger.

The hayloft definitely had potential, but a hiding place must be made discovery-proof. Following the example Father had seen at his sister's, we concocted a plan to build a false wall across the loft, about 3 feet from the front end. This wall must be made to look just like the inside of the outer wall. Yossel, the handyman, commenced construction, with some help from me, Father, and our cousin Issa.

This was a slow, prolonged project, as we first had to scrounge up the bricks and mortar, then smuggle them into the stable. Any sign of this unusual construction project must be concealed, not only from the Nazis, but from the neighbors as well. Although the chance of voluntary betrayal by other Jews wasn't our greatest concern, it was a possibility, and it was best to play it safe. As it turned out, during the final purge, the Nazis did torture many captured Jews to force them to reveal the location of other Jews' hiding places. It was also quite possible that when the critical time came, other families might demand entry, making an already over-crowded space unsurvivable.

By removing a brick from the outside front wall, we could observe what was going on in front of the stable while we were in hiding. For better ventilation, two bricks were made removable, and a foot-square piece was cut out of the roof and saved, so it could be put back in place if it was thought that someone might check the roof. When the wall was completed and plastered over, someone coming into the loft would think he was looking at the back of the outside front wall. A small opening, just large enough to crawl through, was left at the bottom of the wall. We had access to the loft itself by a ladder through a trap door.

One major problem was that it would be impossible to close the hiding place from inside without leaving some sort of obvious telltale sign of the entry hole at the bottom of the wall. This meant that for the safety of those inside the hiding place, someone had to stay on the outside to close it up. I became this someone—the outside man. Once the rest of the family had gotten into the hiding-place, their lives were in my hands. I had to close the entrance, and thoroughly disguise it from inside the loft, which I did by piling old scraps of plywood and boards against it. I would then climb down, take the ladder away, and put it outside in the garden. But then what was I to do?

So in addition to the bunker in the loft, we needed to devise a place for me to hide down below. One of the large wardrobes we had brought from home turned out to be the key. This portable closet was about 6 feet tall and 4 feet wide; at the bottom was a drawer, and the upper part, where clothes were hung, was covered by sliding doors. It stood on four short legs. To create my hiding place, a hole was cut in the wooden floor, smaller than the wardrobe, but large enough for a man to pass through. Then a large space was dug in the ground, big enough for me to lie in with my knees pulled up. The legs were cut off of the wardrobe and it was slid over the hole. From inside the room, it appeared to be a normal closet sitting flush on the floor. To get into my burrow, I would pull out the drawer, part the clothes hanging inside, lower myself into the hole, and slide the drawer in over me.

In addition to our real hiding places, we made a couple of fake hiding-places, poorly disguised, so that it wouldn't be too difficult to discover them. In the garden, some holes were dug, made to look as though someone had been lying in them, and covered with old plywood and dirt. Inside the stable, a poorly disguised trapdoor was made in the wooden floor, with a hole dug out beneath it and covered by a small rug. This trapdoor was only a few feet from where I would be actually hiding under the wardrobe. The hope was, of course, that when the Nazis found these "hiding-places," they would assume the premises had been abandoned. Whether or not this ruse actually came into play will never be known, but it is quite possible that it was another link in that chain of resourceful decisions, combined with great strokes of luck, or miracles, that led to our family's ultimate salvation.

We now felt that we had a fairly good chance to avoid being picked up for transportation, given any advance warning at all. But long-term survival meant that we must eventually find a means to survive outside the Ghetto. This would be tough. Getting out was possible, but how to find a place to live and how to avoid being identified as Jews, that was the sticky part. Somehow, as a first step, we needed to get our hands on new ID papers. The ones we had been issued by the Germans contained not only the fatal word "Jewish" as our religion, but our obvious Jewish names and our former address, which was in a Jewish area of the city. Once again Lady Luck would find her way to the Szpringers. Of course as is usually the case, we had to go out and find her.

On July 30, 1943, as I was carrying water home from the community well, I passed a group of young Jews talking together. Among them was my friend Israel Diamond. I overheard one of them, while looking directly at me, say "He could do it." Now, what was that all about? I wasn't going to let that question go unanswered. I walked a little ways past them, set my buckets down, and waited until the others went away; then I went back to talk to Israel. I asked him what the group had been saying about me. Israel told me that the group felt that I looked Aryan enough to pass as a gentile, if I had the right papers. Furthermore, Israel, who was a chemist, offered to show me a chemical process for removing and replacing names on ID papers. Wow! This might be a life-saver. Israel said that the process was very simple and used easily available household products. Of course, I was more than eager to learn this process, and offered to pay him to teach me. Israel said he didn't want any money, and he would come to our stable tomorrow at noon and show me, but I should be alone; he didn't want anyone else there.

Exactly at 12 o'clock the next day, as promised, Israel showed up, and shared this potentially life-saving gift with me. We began by working on my own ID paper; carefully applying the solution to those parts we wanted to remove—my name, my address in the Jewish neighborhood, my mother's maiden name, and my religion. Very slowly the ink disappeared where we put the solution, and by four o'clock I was ready to write in my new identity. This was fantastic! Now I could change the identities of the whole family.

It took considerable time and very exacting work, but eventually I was able to convert the papers of everyone in the family from Jewish to Polish gentile. We anticipated, and it proved to be true, that in the future still other ID papers with different addresses would be necessary. For this purpose we might steal blank papers or obtain papers from deceased persons, and alter them. For now the major concern was whether my forgeries would pass inspection when presented to authorities. We would get the chance to find out, soon enough.

After much thoughtful consideration, we arrived at a set of new names for our new Polish identities. The names were chosen from familiar names to make them easier to remember, and to increase the chance of pronouncing the new name correctly, without hesitation. Father would no longer be Abraham Szpringer the Jew, but a Pole named "Jan Drzewo." This name was chosen because a cousin had that last name and a first name that started with "J". Jan was a nice short Polish name and drzewo means "tree", so the combination was very easy for him to remember. Mother (Baila) took "Bronslowa" as her first name. Yossel simply used the Polish version of his own name, "Jusek". Laya was called Poilka (we don't know why). Mother, Yossel, and Laya all took the last name "Fletzau" (the name of a Polish doctor we knew in the nearby town of Dombrowa). I became "Mieczyslaw Scrowronski", but would use the familiar form "Mietek". We spent many hours practicing our new names, so that we would come up with them and respond to them instantly in high pressure situations.

How lucky it was that I didn't just walk on and pass off the remark, "He could do it", as insignificant. But it wasn't just luck. By this time we had developed the habit of being keenly alert and gleaning every little bit of information that came our way, and this habit was vital to keep us alive.

Israel Diamond had also given us another extremely valuable bit of advice. He was an active member of a Zionist organization, and in that role he had held retreats in the small resort town of Jelesnia, in the foothills of the Carpathians. He suggested that if my family had Polish papers, we could pretend to be on vacation in Jelesnia for up to two weeks at a time without attracting any special notice. Upon arrival for our "vacation," we would simply register as vacationers at the city hall.

CHAPTER TWELVE

Judenrein
(Told by Laya)

All the while that our family was working on our bunker in the loft, Yossel was also helping the neighbors to construct a hiding place in the cellar under the house in front of our stable. To help conceal the fact that we had our own bunker, he acted as though this would also be our family's primary hiding place, together with the neighbors. Access to the cellar, which was divided into several small rooms, was by way of some outside steps at the rear of the house. Yossel plastered over the doorway between the rest of the cellar and the small room under the front of the house. Now, anyone entering the cellar would think that this plastered over wall was the end of the cellar, and have no clue that a bunker was concealed on the other side. To provide an access to the bunker, the top boards of the front step of the house were pried loose so that they could be lifted up, and the people could crawl in and climb down into the bunker by a short ladder. After the last person had come into the bunker, the boards could be replaced and secured from inside. Once the bunker was ready, all those who planned to use it held several practice drills by opening the step and climbing down into the cellar. This was done, of course, under the cover of darkness.

In the early morning of August 1, 1943, Moishe was taking his turn standing guard, while the rest of us slept our usual restless sleep in the quiet tension of the Ghetto night. The night had been uneventful, like most other Ghetto nights and Moishe was fighting the urge to give in to sleep, when he was suddenly jolted out of his reverie as the darkness of the Ghetto was washed away by total illumination. Giant floodlights lit up the whole Ghetto from all sides, and brilliant, burning flares floated down on us from above. It was so bright that you could pick up a pin on the ground. Moishe immediately woke us up, and we all jumped up, but to avoid being seen we crawled on our stomachs to the house in front, and along with the people from the house, scampered down into the blackness of the bunker, with the exception of Moishe, who took refuge in his hole under the wardrobe. Why didn't we go into our own hiding place in the loft? We were following a pre-planned strategic decision, for at the time we had no way of knowing what the Germans were up to, and we didn't want to prematurely reveal the existence of our own hiding place to the neighbors.

No one doubted that the Nazis had something sinister in mind for us, but we didn't yet know that this was the start of an action to make the Bendzin Ghetto "Judenrein" (Cleansed of Jews)—"the final solution" to the "Bendzin Jewish Problem." Being aware of the Nazis cynical ways, perhaps we should have expected something fiendish on this day, for August 1, in 1942, in the Jewish calendar was the tragic day of Tisch b'Av—the day of the destruction of both the first and the second Temples in Jerusalem.

Altogether, there were about twenty of us crammed into this small bunker—men, women, children, and one tiny baby. Against one wall was a long bench. Those of us who didn't get a seat on the bench tried to make ourselves comfortable on the floor. Had we planned better we would have brought something to cushion ourselves from the cold, hard floor. But with life itself on the line, comfort was way down the list of things on our minds. For now, the darkness was relieved by the light from one small carbide lamp.

As we huddled cowering in this dimly lit chamber of fear, our only shred of comfort came from the close contact with each other, and a feeling of oneness that came from our common danger. We turned off the lamp as soon we could hear the Germans approaching, going from house to house, pounding on doors with rifle butts, demanding, "Alle Juden, raus!" (All Jews, out!), as they swept through the Ghetto, moving ever closer to us. Even more frightening than the screams of the two-legged beasts was the barking and growling of the savage canine beasts who were aiding them in their murderous search. Our disguised refuge might fool the soldiers, but what about these keen scented German shepherds? All the while, sporadic gunfire served as further reminder of the gravity of our situation. We knew that each machine gun burst meant that some Jew, or Jews, had met the violent fate that we were expecting any minute for ourselves.

Our fear was elevated to heart numbing terror as the stomping of these killers' boots on the floorboards overhead penetrated into the chill air of the bunker. More terrifying yet was the scraping of canine claws on the bare boards, as they scrambled through the house. The worst moments were when they stopped. Had they discovered something? Every time they paused, I was sure I could hear them sniffing, and my breathing stopped. When the last of these tormentors left the house, there was a common sigh of relief, but no celebration, not even a silent one, for we all had the feeling that this was just the first phase. We knew that the total illumination of the Ghetto in the middle of the night signaled more than just a partial roundup. Unfortunately we hadn't really prepared for this surprise raid, and certainly not for a prolonged stay in the bunker. No one brought any food or water; we didn't even have a bucket for a toilet. Prepared or not, we had no choice but to stay in the bunker, at least until darkness came again the following night.

At the initiation of this 'action,' many people ran into the adjacent cornfield, in an attempt to hide. Throughout the early morning we could hear long bursts of machinegun fire, as the Nazis sprayed the cornfield. As our friends and neighbors lay unseen between the rows of corn, most were found by the strafing bullets.

The initial roundup took three or four hours, collecting those people who voluntarily surrendered, or those who were poorly hidden. This group comprised the great majority of the Jews still living in the Ghetto. The dawn was now breaking, and some neighboring Poles were able to observe the action in the Ghetto. They later told of seeing long lines of those captured being marched to the rail siding in Bendzin, where cattle cars stood waiting with doors open like the maws of ravenous beasts eager to be stuffed with these pathetic doomed souls. As these helpless Jews were marched, the whole way they were being kicked, whipped, beaten

with rifle butts, and prodded with bayonets, in a display of unnecessary brutality. These unfortunates included small children, and
many aged and infirm, many of whom were so weak from hunger
they could barely walk or had to be held up to walk. Not the slightest hint of mercy was shown to anyone; those who were too slow
were prodded and beaten the whole march as they dragged themselves to the rail siding, which was about two miles away. These poor
wretches were then crammed into the cattle cars, and shipped to
Auschwitz. Just because the Nazis packed the people into cattle
cars, didn't mean that they thought of them as cattle. They would
have treated cattle far more humanely.

More than 8000 innocent men, women, and children were
transported during this roundup. The vast majority were sent directly to the "showers", and murdered upon arrival. One particular car was very rebellious, and gave the Germans a lot of trouble;
somehow, several prisoners had even managed to jump from the
train. When the train pulled into Auschwitz, this car was not un-
loaded like the rest; instead, the Nazis set up machine guns and
slaughtered the prisoners right there in the car.

Our trial by terror had just begun. As we expected, the first
search had barely ended before a new and more determined search
began. Those of us still hiding knew, of course, that our lives depended on our remaining absolutely silent. We had a very serious
problem. There was one mother in the bunker with a small baby.
This baby *absolutely must* be prevented from crying. The mother
had taken the precaution of bringing laudanum drops as a sedative, and had been giving the baby some drops whenever it began
to stir. However, medicine of any kind was very difficult to obtain
in the Ghetto, and she had a very limited amount of laudanum.
After a few hours she had used up all of her sedative, and the infant
began to cry. All of her efforts to quiet the child were in vain, and
everyone in the bunker was becoming quite desperate. All of our
lives were being put at severe risk. The mother was frantic. How
could she be expected bring herself to smother her own baby, but
she knew that was the only option if any of us were to have any
chance to survive. Nearly out of her mind, the mother tearfully
pleaded for somebody to silence the infant. No one wanted to

perform this dreadful duty, but with all of our lives at stake, one man finally took the baby from its mother and smothered it until it was silent. We have a painful sympathy for the person who had the strength to do this deed, for however necessary it was, this person was undoubtedly haunted by the memory of this deed for the rest of his life. For all of the rest of us who lived, this image is deeply engraved in our minds forever—more fuel for our nightmares.

From our hole in the ground we couldn't tell much about what was going on outside. The minutes passed like hours in a state of constant, silent dread, to be punctuated, with no warning, by moments of sheer fright as the beasts of prey and their canine accomplices returned again and again to continue their evil pursuit in the space above our heads. With each violent entry, our breathing was reduced to a near stop, returning to normal again only after their departure. This was an instinctive reaction, not a calculated one, as they weren't likely to have heard our breathing for all their shouting and cursing. After what seemed an endless day, and we had heard no sounds for at least an hour, Yossel loosened the tread of the front step, and very, very slowly raised it up until he could see though a narrow slit, that no one was in sight, and that it was sufficiently dark for us to make an escape. All of us surviving prey had had enough of this tomb and craved fresh air, so we slithered out, and crawled on our stomachs back to our 'homes.' Each family went off in its own direction. We told the others that we planned to hide in the cornfield, which was where many of the others had said that they were going. A few of the others gathered food, water and other necessities, and sought refuge again in that awful cellar, where the memory of the tragically silenced infant permeated the air.

But once back in our stable, we retrieved the ladder from the garden, and climbed up into our small hiding place in the loft, which was to be our home from then on. Moishe then buttoned up the bunker, put the ladder back in the garden, and stood watch in the room below, always ready to dive into his hole beneath the wardrobe. The Germans had apparently suspended the search for the night, probably because, as we learned later, a few young people had obtained guns, and had put up a fight, killing a small number of soldiers. At early light the predators renewed their murderous foray, driving Moishe into his cramped refuge under the wardrobe for the rest of the day.

A serious problem developed that first day that could have had disastrous consequences. Yossel had caught a cold that had developed into an uncontrollable cough. Summoning all his willpower, being fully aware of how our lives depended on complete silence, he was still not able to suppress this cough. When he would start to cough, the other men took the desperate measure of holding a pillow over his face until the coughing ceased. Somehow he survived this ordeal.

The summer heat was stifling, and the seven of us soon used up what little water we had. Our only food was a rucksack full of dry toast that Mother had prepared. However, we thought very little about food. We were too scared to think about anything except avoiding capture. It is impossible to describe what it was like to sit minute after minute, hour after hour, day after day, in this cramped, stuffy coop, in a constant state of fear. Being packed into this sardine can we had made for a bunker, with seven people crammed into a space that would be miserable for one, with only minimal ventilation, and no water, we were prisoners in a living Hell. We were locked into a horrible nightmare from which there was no awakening. We were desperate to go out and search for water, but to venture out was not a sane option. Peering through the hole where the brick had been removed, we could see the Nazi fiends prowling around day and night. Every house and possible hiding place in the Ghetto, including our stable, was being systematically searched.

At every door they yelled, "Juden Raus!" –Jews come out!— then barged in with their guns at the ready. Those Jews who were found, and not shot, were marched to the rail siding, where they were sent directly to Auschwitz. The Germans were now helped not only by dogs, but also by the Jewish Militz, whom the other Jews considered to be lower than dogs. These intense searches went on for about a week, by the end of which the bodies of at least 1200 Jews lay strewn about the Ghetto. The Nazis' persisted in their grizzly "War Against the Innocents" until the end of the war, by which time, it is estimated that less than one per-cent of the Jews of Bendzin were alive. The rest had been converted to ash on the ground and soot in the sky, as an offering to the Nazi Gods of Self-Defined Superiority and Hatred.

Cowering helplessly in our little bunker, what we saw was terrifying enough, but what we heard was even worse: Germans and the hated Militz screaming orders, those horrible dogs growling and barking, the wrenching cries of people being found hiding and being pulled out of their failed refuges, and the sporadic gunfire. Our fear was so intense that we didn't even think about things such as how hungry or uncomfortable we were. Every little movement outside, every little unexpected sound sent a chill through us; if a bird flew close to our bunker, the flutter of its wings made our hearts miss a beat. I don't know how we survived the terror when the persistent predators searched our stable down below. This went on day after day, seeming like an eternity.

Our dreadful thirst was becoming more than we could bear. Bella had saved a small amount of water, which she was dispensing, a spoonful at a time, only to her child, Chana. Mother begged her for just a spoonful, but Bella refused. There was a bitter argument, but Bella would not yield. With no possibility of getting any water, after a day or so our thirst became so unbearable that Mother took a rag and filtered the urine that had been collected in a jar, and out of desperation some of us drank some of it.

After perhaps a week of being trapped in the loft, things slowly began to quiet down to a point where it looked like it might be possible to venture out without being shot, if you were very cautious. Moishe and Yossel took on the risk of making nighttime forays in search of water. They first searched in the house in front, but had no luck. At great risk they worked their way over to the communal well only to find the Germans had closed it. Finally, one night they did find an unused well, from which they could pull up some water in a bucket. Using a long stick with a bucket hooked onto a notch at the end, they were able to pull up a small amount of water. But they were worried about how safe it would be to drink it. They had heard that the Germans had been known to poison wells in other places. They had ample reason to be concerned when they saw that the water had a green scum floating on top. Suffering from severe thirst, Yossel couldn't resist testing the water by taking a few sips. He had slaked his thirst a little, but not long after climbing back into the bunker he came down with a high fever. He survived this very dangerous test, and showed that perhaps the water could possibly be used. Mother found some cotton to make a filter, and slowly poured the scummy water through it. The water looked much better, although far from crystal clear, so we all took a small mouthful. We all knew we were taking a risk, but as parched as we were, we just didn't care. What other choice did we have? To our great relief, none of us became ill. Yossel and Moishe continued to make their nightly forays in search of water and food; sometimes discovering a mud puddle where they were able to collect a few spoonfuls of precious liquid.

In hindsight, we might ask ourselves why we didn't stock the bunker with something as obviously necessary as water, in advance of hiding there. The reason is simple. We must remember that up to that time, we had very little information as to what was happening in the rest of Poland. We weren't aware that the Nazis were systematically making every city and ghetto in Eastern Europe 'Judenrein'. Prior to this Judenrein action, all of the collection of Jews for transportation from Bendzin had been staged in the daytime, and often, an alert person could foresee the danger, and retreat to a hiding place until the collection was finished. Therefore, we were not expecting to use our hiding place as a long-term refuge.

CHAPTER THIRTEEN

Hiding and Capture
(Told by Moishe)

One morning I was sitting in the horse stable looking out the open door while keeping out of sight, when I heard something that set off the danger bell in my brain. Springing into action, I quickly scrambled into my hole under the wardrobe. My hasty retreat was well advised, for no sooner had I scrunched in, than an SS man showed up, accompanied by a Jewish Militz, for the purpose of searching our families' "home." The Militz man found the ladder in the garden, brought it into the stable, and climbed up into the loft. The lives of seven people hiding upstairs in the attic were hanging by a thread behind the pseudo-wall at the end. Those inside their tiny sanctuary could not be sure of what was happening on the other side of the wall, except that whoever was out there was not a friend. Nearly paralyzed with fear, they were quite aware that they must remain absolutely quiet if they were to live though this day, for one sound or a poorly hidden entrance hole, and they would all be summarily shot, or transported to the furnaces of Auschwitz. But the Fates were in our corner this day, for the Militz man didn't detect the cleverly disguised hiding-place. He did, however, find a pair of very fine quality high-top boots that I had attempted to hide in the loft, which he turned over to the SS man. With Death lurking around the corner, his scythe at the ready, the loss of a pair of fine boots was insignificant; but having to lie there, and witness this traitorous Jew collaborating with the Nazis, is something that I will never forget nor forgive.

It was with good reason the SS man sent this Jew into the loft, instead of doing the search himself. The SS were cruel, but not stupid. There were a few cases of the Jews in hiding having guns.

A great many more wanted to go down fighting, but guns were extremely hard to obtain. Indeed, some German soldiers had been killed while trying to flush out the Jews from their bunkers.

Outside the stable we had slapped together a small shed, in which we had stored 30 or 40 pairs of high quality new shoes in gunnysacks, camouflaged with some wood scraps. We had padlocked the door to prevent theft. In hindsight, perhaps we should have left the door unlocked, for a locked door implies something of value inside. Of course, the SS man broke the lock, found the shoes, and took them away. This could have been a disastrous loss for us, as shoes, or any kind of trade goods, were like gold. A fugitive without a means to buy, barter, or bribe, had virtually no chance of surviving, but we were not so naïve as to put all our eggs in one basket–or one gunnysack. We had secreted away other valuables, including another dozen or so other shoes in a better hidden spot in the loft, which the SS man and his Melitz helper did not find. The fake hiding places we had made for the Germans to find were easily located during this search, and those that followed, and they apparently assumed these false hiding places were all there was to find in the horse stable. During all the searches, I would be lying in my hole under the closet with the Germans sometimes only inches away, while the rest of the family were sitting petrified just overhead.

Among the few living creatures in the Ghetto were the birds, so I worked out a treaty with my avian friends whereby I would toss a few bread crumbs on the wooden floor of the stable, and they rewarded me by serving as my sentinels. The birds quickly learned to come in and peck at the crumbs, but if they suddenly stopped and flew away, then I knew that someone was coming and it could only be Germans. I would scramble into my burrow under the wardrobe, and even though I couldn't see anything, I could tell when the Germans were gone because birds would come back and sound the "all clear" by pecking at the floor. An additional benefit was that when the Germans saw birds flying out of the stable it would appear to them that it must be vacant.

My foremost concern, while lying, sometimes for hours, in my dismal hole under the wardrobe, was the safety of myself and my family, but something else, very personal, was also weighing on my mind. Her name was Mania Berkowicz, and I was in love. Mania was a cute little redhead who had worked in our shoe store as a salesgirl. Only the two of us knew how we felt about each other; that's the way it was in those days. She was an only child, who lived with her parents in Groditz, a village on the outskirts of Bendzin, about four kilometers from our shoe store. I used to make up excuses to walk her home whenever I could.

By the time Mania went to the Ghetto she had been orphaned by the gas chambers in Auschwitz. During the day, she worked for Rossner, making clothes, and at night she was staying wherever someone would take her in. The pitiful condition of her life bothered me a lot, and I wanted to do something to give her more security and comfort. It appeared to me that the only thing I could do was to convince her to move into our stable with us. It would be a considerable burden for us to take in another person, especially if and when it became necessary to move into the already overcrowded bunker overhead, but they consented to take her in, if she agreed. As soon as I got the family's consent, I raced off to find Mania. It was already late in the afternoon when I found her, and I had no luck in convincing her to move into our stable that day. Undoubtedly, the chance to greatly improve her living conditions must have appealed to her, but she had been brought up very strictly, and she would just not feel comfortable moving in with her boyfriend in such close quarters. I pleaded with her, but she could only say that she would think about it. Unfortunately, this was the afternoon of July 31, 1943, the last day of existence for the Bendzin Ghetto. I never saw my shy, sweet Mania again.

About ten days after the Judenrein roundup began, Issa Felsensztien made a momentous decision, to leave the bunker and the Ghetto, and take his chances on the outside. He and the rest of us were painfully aware that staying in the Ghetto indefinitely could only lead to being caught and murdered or starving to death. Just that morning we had witnessed an alarming scene. Looking out through the holes we had made in the front wall, we saw a Polish boy, about 12 years old, leading some SS men to the house in front. He was talking to them, and pointing to the upper part of the house. The SS began screaming at the house, and after a few minutes, a trap door in the roof opened and several Jews climbed out with their hands over their heads. They had succeeded in escaping capture far longer than most of the Jews in the ghetto, but were now on their way to Auschwitz.

This incident was a vivid reminder of how precarious our situation was, and the urgency of finding a solution. The only questions, for all of us, were when to leave and where to go. Cousin Issa was more anxious to take his family out, because they didn't have milk or any other proper food for their little Chana, and she was the whole world to them. For some strange reason, he insisted that when the Felsensztien went out, the Szpringers must also go out. We argued at length with him about this, until it was agreed that Father and I would go outside the Ghetto with the Felsensztiens, and then the parties would separate.

The five of us left the stable at about 2 a.m. with our hearts in our throats. Crawling ever so cautiously from one dark spot to the next, it took us nearly four hours to cover the mile or so to the boundary of the Ghetto. Issa had plans to go to a Polish family he knew, and to whom he thought he could entrust the lives of his family. So, off into the darkness went our cousin Issa, the devoted wife and mother Bella, and beautiful little Chana–never to be seen or heard from by us again. Whether or not this Pole that Issa trusted turned them in or not, we will never know. Someone told me after the war that Issa had been seen in Auschwitz. That might be true, but there can be little doubt that Bella and Chana were murdered upon arrival there. Little Chana's beautiful, dark, sparkling eyes didn't charm her heartless murderers.

For our part, Father and I didn't have any definite plan. For us, this was mostly a scouting expedition, because we had no idea what was going on outside the Ghetto. Nothing we did could be considered safe, but we had to take some action soon, as the eastern sky was getting light. We decided to take the risk of going to the house of a Pole we knew, named Jusek. He had worked in the back of our shoe store, repairing shoes for Jarosz, when I was still there. We didn't know him very well, but he had seemed like a decent fellow.

I tapped on the door, and an obviously nervous Jusek and his wife quickly let us in. My father gave them a bottle of vodka and a 2 1/2 meter bolt of fine quality suit material. The Poles were quite surprised to see that we were still alive, but were none too happy to have us under their roof; however, they agreed to let us stay until nightfall. It was time for Jusek to leave for work, so he left the house, giving us his word of honor that he would not betray us. Not long after the sound of his footsteps faded, he was back, with two German policemen. The interrogation began with a demand to see our identity papers, which I had so carefully altered, to prove that we were Polish, but the police were not buying this. When asked who we were, twice I insisted that we were Poles, and twice I was smacked to the floor. I don't why I bothered to pretend to be Polish, since Jusek had certainly told them that we were Jews, and denying it only got me some bruises. Of course, they immediately arrested us. Father pleaded that he be allowed to take a little drink of vodka to settle his nerves before they took us away. One policeman was willing to let him have a swig, but the other vetoed the idea, and they marched us off to the police station.

At the station, the police were not sure what to do with us. A truck had just left for Auschwitz with some captured Jews, so there was now no transportation for these unexpected additional two Jews. This was another Szpringer family miracle, as Father and I would surely have been on that truck had it still been there. But it wasn't, so the Germans decided to return us to the Kamionka. We were also lucky to have been picked up by the Order Police rather than the SS, who would probably have just shot us. Early in the afternoon, we were marched back to what used to be the Ghetto, and turned over to a Jewish policeman, who assigned us to a clean-up crew. There were still a great number of dead bodies to be removed from the streets.

At the end of the workday the German in charge blew his whistle, and assembled the crew. A few Jews, who were new that day, including me, were separated out and marched to Srodula, which was the location of the Sosnowiec Ghetto. I had noticed earlier that Father was nowhere to be seen, but didn't have a chance to look for him.

In Srodula, I found that three of my cousins, Mancha, Riven and Moishe Altman, were still alive and working in the camp kitchen. Of course, the Altman brothers were amazed to learn that all of my family were still alive. Mancha asked me if I wanted any food, but I told him that I didn't. I told him that I was only interested in getting back to Bendzin the next day. I asked Mancha if he could intercede with the Jewish police to make sure that I would be sent back to Bendzin. Mancha agreed that he would try, but also told me that nothing really mattered, because before long, we would all be in Auschwitz. It may appear strange that I would turn down an offer of food, but I had eaten so little for so long that I no longer craved food. At this stage, my mind was totally focused only on my and my family's survival.

That night I slept outside beside one of the buildings. First thing in the morning, I set out to find where the work crew for Bendzin was gathering. Several groups were forming, so I asked a Jewish policeman which group was going to Bendzin. I had no way of knowing if Mancha had talked to anyone on my behalf or not, but this Jew pointed out the crew I should join, and then asked if I were Mancha's cousin. When I told him that I was, he went directly over to the German sergeant in charge of the crew, and told him that I was planning to escape. I was naturally furious that this fellow Jew would betray me, but I was beginning to expect this from the Militz.

The Nazi strode over to me and said, "So, you want to run away!" pointing his Luger in my face. I knew full well that this German could pull the trigger with impunity, if for no better reason than to amuse himself.

"Oh, no" I pleaded, "I give you my word of honor I won't run away."

The Nazi grew red in the face, and snarled, "Since when does a stinking Jew have any honor?"

I assured him that the thought of escape had never even crossed my mind.

"If you're stupid enough to try it, I'll shoot you dead," warned the German, holstering his Luger. As soon as this Nazi put away his pistol, I relaxed; knowing that I was safe, at least for the time being.

"Before you shoot me, you'll have to catch me," I said–to myself.

The first thing I did when the truck got back to the Bendzin Ghetto was to try to find Father. As soon as we were together, I asked him, "Where did you disappear to yesterday?"

Father told me that he had sat down with a group of Jewish workers who were taking a break. Before long, he noticed that without saying a word, one of the men was signaling to another with his eyes. The first one got up and started to walk away, followed by the second man. Father sensed that it might be a good idea to follow them and find out what was going on. As he rounded a building, he caught up with these men just as they were opening up an entrance to a hidden bunker. Since Father was now with them, they pulled him in and closed the entrance, where they all stayed until morning. They had learned from experience that keeping out of sight of the Germans at the end of the workday was always a wise move.

Father and I went back to work in the clean-up crew for the rest of the day, but before the leader blew the final whistle, we had each taken a bucket, as if going for water, and making absolutely sure that nobody observed us, took off by separate routes in the direction of the family stable. I was able to hide in an empty house until dark, but Father was not so lucky. Hearing German voices around the corner, he realized that the only place he could quickly hide was in a latrine, so he went in and closed the door. He then realized the one of the Germans might decide that he wanted to use the latrine. Fortunately, the board with the holes cut in it was not nailed down, so he lifted it up and climbed down into the pit. These soldiers passed by, but no sooner did it appear that the coast was clear than voices of others could be heard. Only after dark did he feel safe to climb out his stinking refuge, and to go back to the stable, where he met up with me.

Together, we slipped into the stable, and so as not to overly alarm those huddled above, tapped lightly on the floor of the bunker, announcing in a hushed voice, "Don't be afraid, it's Moishe and Father." The reality of the situation was that those left behind had little reason to expect to ever see the two of us again, and one might presume that the return of us two intrepid scouts would be cause for a minor celebration, with much embracing and tears; however, no such celebration took place. Although the others were certainly relieved and thankful that we were safe, all of us were much too traumatized by our constant fear to think of anything but staying alive.

The rest of the family were, of course, eager to hear about what was going on outside of our bunker; so Father and I recounted our harrowing experiences during our excursion into the outside world over the last two harrowing days. Nothing that we told them was very reassuring, but the next step was to come up with a plan of action. There was some discussion and speculation as to what the Felsensztiens' fate might be, but dwelling on this topic was a waste of time. We needed to concentrate on our own problems. My first duty was to create new ID papers for Father and me, our first ones being confiscated by the police.

A couple days after returning to the loft, I sneaked over to the house in front, hoping to find something useful, in particular a razor. Luckily, I found an old razor, and was heading back when I heard Yossel, who was watching through the hole in the front wall, calling to me, in a whispered shout, "Look out! Germans coming!" I dashed back, and scrambled into my burrow under the dresser, just in time to elude two Nazis walking past the open door. The door had been kept open since the beginning of Judenrein to give the appearance that the stable was unoccupied.

A day or so later, we heard the sound of hammering that was coming closer and closer to us. When the workers got to our stable, we discovered that they were two Jews, who had been caught in town and brought back to the Ghetto to work. They had been assigned the job of nailing shut all the doors of the abandoned buildings in the supposedly empty Ghetto. This, of course, would leave us with no way to go in and out. Luckily, Father recognized them as former neighbors, and implored them to pass up the stable; which they agreed to do, and went on to the next building. This latter-day version of the Passover by these two "angels" undoubtedly saved our lives, and we deeply appreciated it. Of course, from then on the door had to be kept shut, and my friends, the birds, could no longer help me.

By this time a few Poles were beginning to come back into Kamionka to take over abandoned properties. Our family realized it was becoming increasingly risky to stay in this hiding place in the loft. If someone decided to move into the house in front and checked the stable, that would be the end of us. So, we needed a new strategy. At the present, hazardous as it was, the loft offered a degree of security, but it was clear that we would soon have to trade the limited security of the Ghetto for a more dangerous environment on the outside. Once outside the Ghetto, we would face a whole host of pitfalls. To start with, many Poles were only too eager to denounce Jews to our mutual Nazi masters. Just a glance from a Pole engendered justifiable fear. Poles who had lived closely with Jews all their lives could often tell a Jew from a Pole by his walk, vocabulary, pronunciation, or by any of numerous mannerisms. While still in the Ghetto before Judenrein, I was always thinking ahead, and had already realized that I would be wise to discard my eyeglasses, because Jews commonly wore them, whereas Poles seldom did. As badly as I needed them, I knew that I had to take them off well in advance of any attempt to pass as a Pole, because the marks by my nose from always wearing my glasses would take some time to disappear.

Up to this time, luck had played a larger role in our staying alive than did survival skills, but when we left the Ghetto the balance would shift. On the outside, we would need uncommon luck, but it was also essential to possess exceptional survival instincts and skills. We had to be shrewd planners, quick thinkers, and convincing actors.

Mother, Father, Issa and Moishe, taken about 1923.

Workers at farm in Ottersleben with overseer Herr Schum.
Poilka (Laya) 2nd row, 2nd from left.

Abraham Szpringer (Father) and his sons, Moishe,
Issa and Josef, after the War.

Perla Baila Szpringer (Mother) with Laya and Josef, 1945.

Josef (Yossel) with friend Jacob Birnbaum, and Theo
Lalushna, who helped save the family.

Doris & Moishe in front of entrance to apartment (upstairs)
at 14 Kołłantaja, Bendzin. 2000

Doris in front of the house in Nova Ruda, near Ludwigsdorf,
where the family reunited after the Holocaust.

Doris and Rae at Sarmacia stadium, where the Szpringers
were inexplicably spared. 2002

Doris, shortly after she met Ralph, about 1960.

Doris and Ralph at the Bar Mitzvah for Rae's grandson, 2004.

CHAPTER FOURTEEN

"Vacation"
(Told by Moishe/Mietek)

We needed to come up with a plan of action, immediately. Father and I had been out once, with almost disastrous results. Yet we knew we could no longer just hole up in the loft. After much discussion, we agreed that we should try to follow Israel Diamond's advice, which was to go to Jelesnia, a small resort town in the foothills of the Carpathian Mountains. There, we would register at the town hall, passing ourselves off as Poles on vacation. Father and I would go first, and if we arrived without problems, and Jelesnia appeared to be a safe haven, then I would return to Bendzin the next day, and give the others a signal to let them know that it was probably safe to follow. A predetermined spot outside the Ghetto was selected, which could be seen from the bunker by looking through one of the holes in the wall. If possible, I was to go to this spot exactly at noon and wave a handkerchief to show that the way was clear.

Around two in the morning, Father and I ventured out from the hiding place, hoping for a better outcome than on our last, nearly fatal, excursion. Father knew a coal miner, who lived with his wife in an apartment in company provided housing. Using extreme caution to avoid being observed, we arrived at the apartment at about four in the morning. A very startled wife hurriedly ushered us into the apartment. We gave her a gold coin to help ease her anxiety. Her husband was still at work on the night shift; but he soon arrived home, in a very distressed state. As soon as he had arrived at the apartment building, some neighbors had informed him that there were Jews upstairs in his home. His and his wife's security was seriously compromised. Understandably, he insisted that we leave immediately, which we did, feeling grateful that at least he hadn't brought in the police, as the last Poles had done.

At such an early hour, two men walking around would certainly attract suspicion; therefore we stole down to the river, where we had some chance to keep out of sight. After the sun had been up for a while, we reasoned it would be relatively safe to be seen on the streets, so we split up, and made our separate ways to the train station in Dambrowa, about four kilometers away, where we bought tickets and climbed aboard a train to Jelesnia.

Luck was again smiling on us, for we arrived at our destination without incident. The first challenge was to find a family who was willing to rent us a room; which took the better part of the day. Eventually we found lodging at a farm on the edge of town, and as it was too late to register with the city, we settled in for the night. The first thing in the morning, we headed for the city hall, and registered as Poles from Bendzin on vacation.

But all these arrangements had taken so long that I wasn't able to return to Bendzin at the prearranged time to give the rest of the family the all-clear signal. After waiting another day, without any contact from me, those in the loft elected to take the plunge, and attempt the escape to Jelesnia on their own. Rather than slipping out under cover of darkness, you might say they borrowed a page from Poe's "The Purloined Letter," and boldly walked out in broad daylight. They had observed that the guard post, which they could see through their small hole in the wall, was usually vacant at noon, so they chose this time to make their break. Having not discovered any Jews in the Ghetto for some time, the Germans had undoubtedly assumed that they had captured all of them, and they were not as vigilant as before, which gave my family a much-needed advantage. Dressed, as best they could like Polish farmers, they loaded the shoes and whatever other trade goods they had left into gunnysacks, and filled the top of the sacks with ears of corn. Taking along a few garden tools to complete the disguise, they walked out from the stable. As if running the gantlet of real or imagined unseen eyes through this Ghetto of carnage was not enough of a daunting trial of courage, we must remember that Mother and Laya had been confined to the cramped bunker, with little food or drink, and virtually no exercise for about three weeks. It took extraordinary mental and physical effort just to put one foot in front of the other. Somehow, they summoned the strength to keep moving, and made it all the way out of the Ghetto without being accosted. The Szpringer's streak of luck was still running.

Just as Father and I had become Jan and Mietek, the minute they stepped out of the stable, the rest of our family was transformed into a Polish family, with new Polish names. They were now Bronslowa, Jusek and Poilka Fletzau. It was essential that all of us new Poles must speak only Polish, even in our most private moments, when we were sure that no one else could hear us. Anything that might be interpreted as Jewish, including any form of prayer, had to be expunged from our lives. From then on, if one of us let slip a Yiddish word, the others became very upset, and strongly reminded the offender that this was a serious mistake; such a careless mistake had the potential to cost us our lives. Jusek got very upset with Mother one time, when she attempted to offer a prayer, by lighting two matches, in lieu of candles, under a table.

So like Father and I had just done, Jusek took his mother and sister to the train station to catch a train for Jelesnia. The usual vacation period was two weeks and therefore anything longer would arouse unwanted interest in them. So we knew that after two weeks we would have to move elsewhere so as not to call attention to ourselves. We didn't know what would happen after the two week "vacation" was over, but Jelesnia was the best option we had for now.

Once out of the ghetto, Jusek headed for the home of a woman he knew and felt he could trust. Mother and Poilka waited off to the side in an inconspicuous spot, while Jusek went to the house. Luckily the woman was home, and my brother asked the woman if she would go to the train station, and buy tickets for them to Jelesnia. She agreed to do so, and they set off for the station, with Mother and Poilka following at a distance so it wouldn't appear as though they were all together. The woman bought the tickets for them, and they safely boarded the next train for Jelesnia.

Walking into the town, they had not gone more than a block or two when they recognized a familiar figure coming in their direction. It was none other than me, coming to see who might be arriving on the train. Without displaying any emotion, we passed each other with a very brief exchange of words; the newcomers moving on to locate a place to stay. Trading their habitat of several weeks in the cramped, stifling, constantly threatening, atmosphere of the loft for their present location in a resort town in the green Carpathian foothills, might be compared to being transported from Hades to the Elysian Fields. However, we were all still living in a constant state of fear, and much too preoccupied with simply surviving, to fully enjoy the beauty of our new surroundings.

For the next two weeks, Father and I didn't venture far from our lodgings, and had no more contact with the other family members. Then Father moved in with another family, on another farm, and I began a series of excursions back and forth to the Bendzin area. I would take the train to Katowice, then on to Dambrowa or Bendzin, but never to Bendzin until after dark, for fear of being recognized, and I never bought tickets at the Bendzin station. I would spend the night in abandoned Jewish houses in Bendzin, because I knew my way around this area. These trips served a dual purpose. Firstly, it kept me active, which helped to reduce my gnawing anxiety. More importantly, if the family stayed too long in Jelesnia, the locals might begin to wonder what they were doing there. I needed to aggressively seek a more permanent sanctuary.

On returning to Jelesnia, I would visit Father at the farm where he was staying, not as his son, but as a friend. One day I accompanied this farmer up into the hills, where he was keeping some cattle. I watched as the farmer opened the barn door, which was barred from the inside, by inserting a thin sliver of wood through a crack and lifting up the bar. This was useful information to me, so I went back to the barn that evening, and spent the next three days there. It was a safe and secluded hiding place, but it was cold at night and all I had to eat were some dried mushrooms.

One morning I decided to explore the surrounding area. While walking along a path, whom should I run into, but Jusek and Poilka. We were all delighted to see each other still alive and well, but I got a little upset as I realized they were spending their "vacation," staying in a nice warm house with plenty of good food, while I was sleeping in a freezing barn, eating mushrooms. I felt a little better, and accepted the disparity in our conditions after they gave me some food. We proceeded down the path together, until we were confronted by two uniformed police officers, who stopped us. They asked us for our papers, and questioned us as to our reason for being where we were. By this time it had become second nature for Jusek and me to have a good story ready at all times. Fortunately, the police bought our story and the validity of our papers, and simply told us to go back to town.

On several occasions Jusek or I, more often Jusek, would have Poilka accompany us when walking about the countryside. As well as police, there were numerous partisans roaming about in the surrounding forest, and whereas a man alone could easily be taken to be an enemy either by the Germans or the partisans, and shot first and questioned later, a man accompanied by a fourteen-year-old girl would appear comparatively innocent.

The morning after our chance meeting, Jusek and I started out together on a trip to Bendzin. On the way to the train station I had an urgent call of nature, likely a result of my mushroom diet. While I slipped off to take care of business in the bushes, Jusek continued on by himself, and was soon stopped and interrogated by a policeman. He was able come up with a story that satisfied the officer, and proceeded down the road to the station. I later joined him, but was still sick and threw up before boarding the train. Had the two of us been together when stopped by this officer, we would have aroused more suspicion, and been put under much closer scrutiny, and very likely would not have been so casually allowed to go on our way.

Late that night, after spending the day in Katowice, Jusek and I were walking through the streets of Bendzin on our way to an abandoned house we had chosen as our refuge until morning. Rounding a corner, we were suddenly startled by the sight of two German policemen on the same sidewalk, maybe thirty feet in front of us. To abruptly turn around and head the other way would have aroused suspicion. All we could do was to brush right past them, trying not to display any signs of nervousness. Amazingly, the officers were not in an inquisitive mood, and ignored us. Sometimes boldness pays off. The more likely scenario would have been for the police to not only ask for our papers, but to demand an explanation of where we worked and what we were doing out so late at night. Had our explanations not been completely convincing, we would have found ourselves in the police station facing a more intense grilling, and very likely given a free ride to Auschwitz.

CHAPTER FIFTEEN

A Lucky Lunch in Dambrowa
(Told by Moishe/Mietek)

One day, I was having lunch in the railroad café in Dambrowa, trying to keep as low a profile as possible, when a young woman, who was a total stranger, walked over and sat at my table. She leaned over to me, and in a low voice stunned me with, "I know who you are. You're Moishe Szpringer." My heart nearly froze, as I wondered how much trouble I was in; but my breathing came back almost to normal when she confided, "Don't worry, I'm Jewish too." I was not only relieved, but excited to find out that there were other Jews still alive and at large. The girl asked me if I would buy her something to eat, which I gladly did. She told me that she was waiting for her brother, whom she expected to arrive on the train in a few minutes. Her brother, she said, could provide me and my family with very valuable papers that could save our lives. My ears perked up at this. This could be the break I'd been praying for, but by now I had enough experience to proceed with caution, and not get too hopeful. I told the girl she should go outside and wait for me. I sat there sipping my coffee, pretending to be nonchalant, until the train came, and then paid my bill to the café manager, who warned me, "Be careful, that girl you were talking to is a Jew."

It was good to find at least one Pole who didn't jump at the chance to turn in Jews to the Nazis. Was it his concern for the girl, or his hatred of the Nazis that led him to not report her? Apparently, his level of caring for her didn't go so deep as to stop him from exposing her to me, a stranger, who very well might have turned her in. In any event, it was reassuring to me that my own efforts to pass as a gentile were succeeding—so far.

Outside the café, I found the girl standing with a young man, whom she introduced to me as her brother Sol, and then she walked off, leaving the two of us alone. I never saw this remarkable girl again and never even asked her for her name, nor do I have any idea how she had survived Judenrein. Sol asked me how many of my family were still alive and free. I told him that I had a father, mother, sister, and brother. Sol found it hard to believe so many from one family could have escaped capture, but he quickly got down to business in a very unemotional manner.

"I can do something for you, and your brother and sister, but your parents will have to go where my parents have gone."

This statement really bothered me; the commandment, "Honor thy Father and thy Mother" immediately popped into my mind. I strongly disliked having anything to do with a man who could speak so unfeelingly of the death of his parents, and who would assume that I would have such callous disregard for my own parents, but it was imperative that I find out more about Sol's scheme.

Sol went on to explain that for the right price—a very large sum of money–he could supply me with two sets of counterfeit papers. The first one would verify that the holder was employed by such and such factory, in another town; the second would state that the holder was on temporary layoff for two weeks due to material shortage. The employment document required a photo of the holder, and both of these documents would require an authentic looking rubber stamp bearing the name of the company that we supposedly worked for. This stamp would be the most difficult thing to obtain. I quickly realized that such papers could very well be the lifesavers I had been looking for. Immediately they would be extremely valuable for me and Jusek, and in turn would greatly enhance our chances to save Mother, Father, and Poilka. I not only didn't like Sol, but was hesitant to trust him, so I told him that I would have to talk it over with my family. Before parting we made arrangements to get in touch, if my family wanted to take advantage of his offer.

As soon as had Sol left, Jusek, who had been watching from across the street, came over to me. He, of course, was anxious to learn the details of what this encounter was all about, but not before admonishing me, "You shouldn't be seen with that girl, she walks like a Jew."

In those desperate circumstances, Jusek and I had to watch our every move, every second of the day. There was absolutely no room for any unnecessary chances. All it would take was one careless mistake and that would be the end of the line. There is no doubt that this extreme caution that we practiced was an essential link in our chain of survival. Sometime these links were a blessed gift, but many times we had to forge them ourselves.

Jusek and I considered ourselves to be pretty resourceful guys, so when we put our heads together we figured that if Sol could make false papers, there was no reason we shouldn't give it a try. Reasoning that many smaller firms must purchase standard employment forms, rather than pay a printer, we sought out a stationery store in Katowice. We were right, and we had little trouble finding the appropriate employee form, purchased a few copies, and then set off for the photo booth in the train station, where we took our pictures. The next step was to select a name of a small manufacturing firm in another town from the phone book, and fill in the blanks. We purposely left off the phone number of the company, because anyone could too easily pick up a phone and discover that the paper was a fraud.

This document was now complete except for the necessary rubber stamp with the name and address of the factory. Obviously, the rubber stamp would have to be manufactured. Equally important was the "layoff" paper, which would explain to any inquisitive policeman why we were walking around in another town, instead of being at work. This could simply be a typewritten sheet of plain paper stamped with an official looking rubber stamp. Getting this paper typed and laying our hands on the rubber stamp were formidable challenges, but we had no choice other than to press on. What we needed was another minor miracle, such as had kept us alive thus far. We would come by it in a rather peculiar way and place, but miracle seekers can't be choosey.

On a subsequent visit to Katowice, while hanging around the train station waiting until after dark to catch the train to Bendzin, we decided to make a visit to the restroom. The fortuitous timing of our arrival in this smelly facility would yield us the minor miracle we so badly needed. While standing at the urinal, I glanced to my left, and what I saw put me in total alert mode. Keeping my face turned to my right, I gave Jusek a slight nudge and signaled with my eyes that he should look at who was standing to my left. Why he had not seen either Jusek or me I'll never know, but right by my left elbow stood Theo Lalushna. This was our first contact with Theo since the previous winter, when he had lost the shoe store to the Romanian, and we were not sure whether he would be friend or foe. Turning us in to the authorities would bring him sizable credit with them, whereas befriending us would put him at considerable risk. Should we attempt to slip out before he spotted us, or take a chance and speak to him? This was a critical decision, but it had to be made instantaneously. We knew the gravity of the predicament we would put Theo in if we approached him, but he had always been kind to us and we felt that he was a good man, so with no more that a knowing nod we agreed to take the chance that he would not betray us. I caught the eye of a visibly surprised Theo, and nodded my head toward the door, as a sign that he should follow us out.

As we reentered the fresh coal-smoke-laden air of Katowice, Jusek and I sensed that Theo appeared to be genuinely concerned about us. As I walked along the sidewalk with Theo, Jusek strolled some ten paces behind. We always kept in mind how important it was for at least one of us to remain alive and free to help the rest of the family survive; therefore, we usually tried to appear as though we were not together, thereby increasing the chance that one of us would escape if the other were caught.

With clearly genuine interest, Theo asked me, "Do you need money?"

"No." (I still had a fair number of those gold pieces we had so wisely hoarded.)

"Do you need food?"

"No."

Theo then inquired, "Where have you been eating?"

Lately I had been going into the Savoy Hotel, a high-class establishment by Katowice standards, for lunch and occasionally for dinner. I had noticed that a large number of German officers frequented this place, often bringing or meeting women there to dine and dance. When I revealed this to Theo, his jaw dropped, he looked right at me, and responded with, "You damned fool! Are you plain crazy!? Don't you have enough trouble without looking for it? Don't you know that Gestapo headquarters are in the Savoy?"

After he cooled down, Theo offered me the name and location of a much safer and cheaper restaurant. Then he asked me how he could help us. I told him that what we needed most was a rubber stamp for some documents. Theo was willing to try to help us, but was becoming increasingly concerned about being seen with us in public, and was anxious to part company; so he suggested that we meet him at his sisters' apartment in Bendzin the following evening At this point I wasn't sure if I could completely trust Theo, so I told him that Jusek and I were close with the partisans, and if anything happened to us, Theo would have a bullet in his head within 48 hours. Of course, this was pure bluff and Theo probably knew it.

Theo lived in a three-story apartment building on Małachowska Street. His rooms were on the third floor, while his two sisters lived together on the second floor. Both sisters had husbands in the German army. At the start of the war, Theo and the younger sister had been living with their parents in Trzebin, a small city about half way between Katowice and Krakow. The older sister, Frau Schultz, had been working in Germany, doing menial labor. After Theo was given several stores in Bendzin, he induced his sisters to join him, so they could all live off the fat of the land together.

With considerable trepidation we cautiously approached Theo's home the next evening. Although we felt that Theo was an ok guy, we also could not ignore the fact that he would benefit much more by turning us in than by helping us. After making sure that the coast was clear, I went up to the sisters' apartment, while Jusek waited in the shadows outside. Theo was shrewd enough to avoid letting me into his own apartment. If the police had followed me, it would be easy enough to concoct a story explaining why a man had gone to a woman's place; whereas, if I were found in Theo's own apartment, it might possibly spell disaster for both of us.

Getting immediately down to business, I provided Theo with the name and address of the company to put on the rubber stamp, and explained that I also needed the "layoff" documents. Theo felt confident that he could have the stamp ready for us the next evening, and Frau Schultz volunteered to type up two copies of a letter stating that the named employee was temporarily laid off for two weeks due to lack of materials. When all these papers were authenticated with the "official" stamp, Jusek and I would be much, much safer moving about the country. By helping us at all, Theo would probably have been shot had the Germans discovered his activities. Although our family did give him some gold, he never asked for it unless it was needed to buy something for us. There is no doubt that Theo was motivated primarily by compassion. There is certainly no question but that he saved our lives, and all of us have always felt very strongly that he was our hero. He also saved several other Jews during these times.

Certainly, possessing the forged papers which Theo helped us acquire was by itself a great asset, but Jusek and I were still in constant danger. While walking around in Bendzin we could be betrayed at any time by some anti-Semitic Pole, but in an unfamiliar town in Poland, where we didn't know our way around, we would stand no chance at all. So we had to use Bendzin, Katowice and Dambrowa as our base. It is probably not possible for anyone who hasn't experienced this kind of life to even begin to realize what it was like for us to live in constant fear, to be a hunted animal, to have to plan every small daily task, such as eating, washing, shaving, cleaning clothes, without even a permanent roof over our heads. Just walking around without appearing nervous or out of place, so as to not attract attention was risky and a daunting challenge in itself. Every waking minute we had to be on guard, and we were not even safe when asleep. Our major problem was that none of our family had been able to visualize any kind of a long-range plan for survival. We were simply "hanging on" from day to day, praying for the war to end, or that some solution, some opportunity, would present itself.

While waiting for a better opportunity for a permanent solution other than the gas chambers, Jusek and I continued to travel back and forth between Jelesnia and Bendzin. On one of these trips, I alighted from the train at Jelesnia, and started walking. I hadn't gone far when a policeman, who was riding on a stagecoach, accosted me. This was not, by the way, like an Old West stagecoach, but rather like a small-wheeled wagon with a canopy over it. The policeman was not satisfied with my papers, so he ordered me to go to the police station and wait for him. Perhaps this policeman recognized that I had been there too many times even though I was not a resident of the place. Since a police station was the last place I wanted to be, as soon as the policeman was out of sight, I hopped aboard the first train back to Katowice. I continued to return to Jelesnia from time to time, but always kept a sharp eye open for this particular cop.

CHAPTER SIXTEEN

Poilka Gets a Job
(Told by Laya/Poilka)

Mietek and Jusek's trips to Jelesnia continued, but our family had been in Jelesnia past the normal vacation season, and we were beginning to sense that the locals were getting suspicious. Jusek was intensifying his search for a new location for us. One fateful day, he returned to Jelesnia to find Mother in tears. She told him that our Polish landlord had told her that someone in town had told him that he was keeping Jews in his house. Naturally, Mother was in a panic. She had no choice but to stay there, waiting for Jusek to return, expecting any minute for the police to show up at her door. When Jusek got home, he calmed Mother down, and went into action. He had learned that sometimes the best defense is a good offense. He had Mother and me pack all our things, and assuming an air of indignation, confronted the landlord. He told the landlord that he and his mother were very upset and insulted that he had been spreading these lies about them. They were moving out, but the first thing they were going to do would be to go to the police and have him arrested for spreading lies about them. He would probably be deported to a work camp. Jusek and Mother, leading me by the hand, stomped out of the house, with the landlord pleading with us not to report him, as he had only repeated what he had heard. Not surprisingly, we went to the train station rather than the police station.

Jusek was too shrewd to just pack up and storm out of our house in Jelesnia unless he had some idea about where to go next. Frau Schultz had given Jusek the name and address of some friends, the Hlinkas, who lived near Cieszyn, a small city on the Polish-Czech border. She felt that, with an introduction from her, these people would help them, as long as they were unaware that we were Jews. Consequently, Jusek took Mother and me to the Hlinka's home, where we were treated very hospitably, and the three of us stayed overnight. Jusek explained to them that our family, who had many children, had lost our home in the invasion, were having great difficulty providing for the children, and needed to find temporary homes for them. I was old enough to work for my keep, and would they perhaps know of a family with whom I might stay and work. The Hlinkas suggested a nearby farm, owned by some good folks by the name of Dzielinski, who might be able to help us. So Jusek took me to the Dzielinski farm, while Mother waited at the train station. The Dzielinskis agreed to take me in, but could only provide room and board in return for my services. This was plenty good enough for Jusek, who left me there, and returned to the station. Much as Mother and Jusek both abhorred the idea, they couldn't come up with any better option than to take Mother back to the miserable hiding place in Kamionka. But at least I had a better arrangement. So Mother returned once again to the loft, while Jusek continued to search for a realistic means for our family to survive long term.

At about this time, Mietek and Father, completely unaware of what had happened to Jusek, Mother, and me, spent the afternoon walking in the forest near Jelesnia. Before returning to the place where Father was staying, Mietek left him to catch the train back to Katowice. On his way back home, Father was surprised by two German policemen walking on patrol. After checking his I.D. papers, they escorted him back to the farm house where he was staying, to verify that he was in fact staying there. They were not completely satisfied with his story, especially since he displayed considerable nervousness, but since they had to finish their patrol, they ordered him to report to the police station in half an hour. Seeing the police escort Father back to the house unnerved the farmer considerably. After the police left, he told Father that he had heard him speaking some strange language in his sleep, and that he wanted Father to find another place to stay. He had probably sensed that Father was a Jew, but didn't want to find out. Father, who needed no urging, straight away threw his stuff into a bag, made a beeline to the train station, jumped onto the next northbound train, and beat a retreat back to the horse stable in Kamionka, where he received quite a shock when he climbed up to the hiding place and found Mother there without Jusek or me.

Soon Jusek came back as well to look after Mother and was, of course, surprised himself to find Father there. He promised our parents that he would come back to the hiding place at least every few days. But still, the situation seemed more hopeless with every passing day. Ever since the German invasion Father had become increasingly depressed. The brief interlude of semi-freedom in Jelesnia had given him some relief, but the return to the hiding place exacerbated his feelings of hopelessness and helplessness to the point that he could no longer summon up any will to carry on. His last close call in Jelesnia was the final straw. Despite Jusek's assurances, he became convinced that his sons would never return. In a state of complete despair, he confessed to Mother that he could not go on any longer and was going to commit suicide. He even went so far as to say his last prayers. Mother pleaded with him to change his mind, but he would not be dissuaded. She begged him to think about her and her situation. She couldn't even bury him. She would have to stay alone in this tiny bunker with his body. This would be more than she could bear, and she would have to kill herself too. After much tearful imploring, she persuaded him to wait one more day, to see if their sons would come back. She conceded that if they didn't show up on the following day, she would not try to stop him from doing whatever he felt he must do. As it turned out, Jusek and Mietek had gotten back together and returned to the stable the next day. By agreeing to wait one more day, Father spared his life, and probably Mother's also. But even so, Father told Mietek that he could not bear to sleep in the bunker anymore. As he put it, "All I see before my eyes is Death."

Father insisted that he wanted Mietek to take him out of the ghetto, and find him some other place to sleep. One problem was that Mietek was spending his nights in abandoned houses with broken windows and no heat, and with winter fast approaching, he knew that Father could not survive the cold. Mietek came up with a possible solution. He remembered that a Polish girl, who

used to work for them in their shoe store, had taken over the operation of a dry-cleaning shop up the street from their store. They
knew her to be a kind-hearted person, so they decided to visit
her at her shop just before closing time, when it would be almost
dark. Following our usual practiced caution, Father suggested
that he go first, and Mietek should trail behind at a safe distance.
They hoped she might allow Father to sleep in the shop after she
closed up.

Arriving at the shop as planned, Mietek waited across the street
while Father went in to talk to the girl. He was greatly pleased,
and appreciative, that she agreed to let him stay there at night.
She and he both knew that she would be putting her life and liberty at extreme risk. No sooner had Father crossed the road to
where Mietek was waiting in the dark, to share the good news with
him, than they observed someone running up the street to the
cleaning shop. It was just light enough for them to recognize the
man as Josef Jarosz. Apparently, somebody had seen Father go into
the cleaning shop, and had told Jarosz, who hustled over there in
great anticipation of catching him and turning him over to the
Nazis. His motivation can't be known for certain, but it is quite
possible that Jarosz was fearful that if any of the Szpringers survived, we might take our store back if the Germans lost the war,
and/or exact revenge on him for his mistreatment of us. Needless
to say, Father's hopes to sleep in the cleaning shop were dashed,
and he had no choice but to return to his gloomy hiding place in
the loft once again.

Meanwhile, I had been having more than a little trouble of
my own in adjusting to life on the farm. Early the first morning,
right after milking, Mr. Dzielinski told me to go out to the stock
pen, open the gate to the pasture, and let the cows out to graze.
As soon as the gate was opened, the cows took off in all directions.
Now, I was a city girl, and was lucky to even know which end of the
cow to feed, so I pretty much panicked, and started running after
them, but it was obvious that I had totally lost control of them. I assumed it was my job to keep them together, and was sure that when
they scattered they would get lost, and I would be blamed. My life
depended on this job, and I would surely lose it. If they threw

me off the farm, how could I survive out in the world by myself? Overcome by hopelessness and misery, I just started walking in no special direction. I hadn't gone far when I came across a group of stones set in the ground. As I walked by, I noticed some faint Hebrew writing on these stones, and I realized that I had come upon a very old, abandoned Jewish cemetery, with mostly cracked and broken stones. I dropped to my knees in front of the graves, and began to cry. Uncontrollably sobbing, I went from grave to grave, and pleaded with those beneath the stones to help me:

"I want to pray, but I don't know how. I don't know what words to use. Pray for me, please. I'm all alone. I don't know if I will ever see my family again. I've been put in this job, but I don't know what I'm supposed to do. If they turn me out, I can't survive. Please, please, help me."

After sitting there weeping for I don't know how long, I gathered myself together, and accepted that I had no choice but to go back to the house and confess to Mr. Dzielinski that I had lost all of his cows, and take my punishment. Mr. Dzielinski just laughed, and told me not to worry; the cows would come home by themselves in time for milking.

But this was not the end of my problems. Almost any job they gave me, I had no experience with, and was too weak to perform well, as I hadn't fully regained my strength after starving in the Ghetto. When Jusek came, after about a week, to see how I was doing, I begged him to find me another place to work. I tearfully protested that the work was much too hard for me, and I was afraid the Dzielinskis were not satisfied with my work, and might just turn me out at any time. Since he had considered it a near miracle to find me this job, he was not very pleased at the prospect of having to find me another place, but Jusek loved his little sister and felt sorry for me, so he agreed that he would do his best, and would be back in a few days. True to his word, in a few days Jusek returned. With the help of the Hlinkas he had found another family in Cieszyn, where the work would be less strenuous. To justify taking me away, his story to the Dzielinskis was that our mother had found a place where she could take care of me, and she wanted her daughter to be with her. He said that I was really sorry to go, and we both thanked the Dzielinskis for taking such good care of me. As a matter of fact, the Dzielinskis were not as displeased with my work as I had imagined, and were genuinely sorry to see me leave.

Since he was not expected to deliver me to the new family (the Unuckas) for another day, Jusek took me back with him to Bendzin, where we met Mietek. After dark we went to our old apartment building at 14 Kołłantaja. As we always did, the three of us walked separately, so as to not appear to be connected. Our building, once so alive with Jewish families and bustling activities, was totally deserted, except for one unit by the front entrance, where a single light was burning. The caretaker Juskowa, who had felt she should have been given our shoe store, was apparently still living there. One by one, we stealthily slipped to the back of the complex, and entered the former home of the Zombeks.

Mr. Zombek, the head of this very pious family of seven, supported them by making buttonholes. We used to tease one of their teenage sons who, because of his piety, never looked at girls. After the Germans came, Mr. Zombek, fearful of being singled out, tried to hide his long beard by covering it with a scarf or collar, and did his best to avoid any contact with them. But the Nazis murdered the whole family.

Mietek had somehow taken possession of a large carp, and was trying to find some way to cook it. Since building a fire of any sort might give away our presence, cooking was simply out of the question, so we decided to temporarily hide it in the wall behind some loose bricks. Mietek also had a few pairs of shoes, which he hoped to sell; these were also hidden in a hole in the wall. We put back the bricks to cover the holes, and went to sleep. Getting up before dawn, we left, one by one, as we had when we came in. Mietek was the last to leave, but before he got to the street, he was caught by Juskowa. She told him that he had no business coming in there, and if she caught him again she would report him to the police. He swore to her that he would never come back, and thanked her profusely for not reporting him. But he really needed the shoes he had stashed, so he took a chance, and came back again that night. Taking chances was nothing new to Mietek. Taking chances had become his way of everyday life. When he slipped back into the Zombek apartment, he found that the shoes, and the carp, were gone. Chalk one up for Juskowa. He sneaked out very early in the morning to assure a clean get-away.

Feeling lucky to have survived the one night in the Zombek's former apartment, Jusek and I had gone back to Cieszyn, where he had taken me to the home of the Unuckas, my new employer—of course I would receive no money. Emil Unucka, the father, worked for the railroad, and was away from home a good part of the time. The Unuckas lived just across the border in Czechoslovakia and were Czech, rather than Polish, which was a huge break for me, as they were less likely to notice any Jewish accent in my Polish.

There were five Unucka children, ages six through twelve, and my job was to take care of these kids, including getting them cleaned and dressed for school. I also did everything else that needed to be done about the house, including washing floors, sewing, peeling potatoes, washing and hanging clothes, and stripping goose feathers for down. Although the Unuckas treated me well, they never led me to feel that I was anything but a servant; certainly not one of the family.

I was given about the same portions of food as the children, but since I worked very hard and for long hours, I was always hungry. I didn't dare complain or ask for more, like Oliver Twist, for fear of jeopardizing my job, but when I could, I did manage to supplement my diet on the sly. For example, the family had a hutch in their backyard where they raised a few rabbits, and since I did all the work around the house, of course, I also fed the rabbits. The rabbits were fed mostly table scraps. Sometimes the bunnies would get short-changed, because I would pick through the scraps and eat whatever I felt was edible.

The house was comprised of two rooms, a bedroom, and a large room that served as kitchen, dining room, and living room. I slept in a large bed in the bedroom alongside the parents, while the kids slept on cots in the kitchen. When Jusek visited, he and I both slept in the kitchen. But his visits were not without their problems. As a result of his fugitive lifestyle, Jusek had considerable problems with personal hygiene. After he left, everyone was scratching from louse bites. It didn't take the Unuckas long to figure out where the lice came from. Mrs. Unucka firmly let me know that Jusek could visit, but definitely could not sleep there anymore.

I got a chilling reminder of how my life hung by a thread when, one morning, Mrs. Unucka informed me that in the middle of the night she had overheard me talking in my sleep. She couldn't understand what I was saying, but it sounded like some language other than Polish. Oh my God! I had never expected this. I was thrown into near panic, but I tried to stay as calm as I could, and pretended to be completely puzzled, insisting that the only language I knew was Polish. All of my self-training to speak only Polish had not converted my unconscious mind, which still operated in Yiddish, and I was in grave danger of discovery even in my sleep. Since I was doing all of their household chores in return for a little food, it is unlikely that the Unuckas wanted to know too much about my background. It is uncertain whether or not the Unuckas would have reported me to the authorities had they discovered I was a Jew, but without a doubt, they would have at least forced me to leave. According to Nazi decrees and practice, being caught harboring a Jew invariably led to severe punishment, such as being sent to a labor camp, or quite often, execution of the whole family.

CHAPTER SEVENTEEN

Frau Shultz to the Rescue
(Told by Moishe/Mietek)

As a result of my rendezvous with Theo at his sisters' apartment, Theo had agreed to meet from time to time with me or Jusek primarily to provide us with cash and coupons in exchange for gold. We would meet in a small park up the street from Theo's home, always after dark, and after each liaison, a time would be set for the next meeting. The coupons were essential, as they were the only way for us to obtain bread. We would tender them in Katowice or Dambrowa, but never in Bendzin, where we might be recognized.

In spite of the obvious risks, Frau Schultz seemed to enjoy our visits to her home, especially when Jusek went there. Her husband was in the army on the Russian front and she was lonely woman. Jusek was a very handsome young man, and on one of his visits Frau Schultz became very aggressive and they ended up rolling on the bed. Whether he wanted this or not, only Jusek knows for sure, but he claims, "She raped me."

Occasionally I would spend the night in Theo's sisters' apartment, which was much better than hiding in some cold abandoned house, but one day Frau Schultz informed me that I could no longer stay there. It seems that she was willing to face the severe consequences of harboring a Jew, but the lice that I was bringing in with me were infesting her home, and that was more than she could bear. These disgusting little creatures, which were just one of the many ancillary torments resulting from our family's way of life, strangely enough became one more important link in our family's survival chain. Having to refuse me the use of her home, prompted Frau Schultz to suggest a plan which, as it turned out, lead us to a momentous decision that would be our salvation. Occasionally we should look back, and say a prayer of thanks for my disgusting little vermin.

Before the war, Frau Schultz had worked on a farm near Magdeburg, Germany, a city on the Elbe River, about 80 kilometers west of Berlin. Because of the war, there was a severe shortage of farm labor; therefore, she felt certain that if my family could get into that region, they could pass themselves off as Poles fleeing from the war zone, and easily find work. Even if an employer were a little suspicious of our papers, it would behoove him to look the other way. She gave me detailed directions as to the best route. First, we should take a train to Magdeburg, and then catch a small local train to Moeckern (about 25 km east of Magdeburg). From there we should walk through the small village of Luehe to the even smaller village of Tryppehna. There were many large farms around there, and we should have no trouble in finding work on one of them.

This suggestion really intrigued me right away. Could this be just the break we had been desperately seeking? I brought this plan to the rest of the family, and everyone was eager to give it a try. We decided that Father and I should go first, and if all went well, we would send word back to Jusek, who would bring Mother and Poilka. One big problem was that the papers we were carrying, with a Bendzin address, would not pass muster with the inquisitive police we were bound to encounter. These papers worked well while we were in the present area, but we needed new ones to use on the way to and inside Germany that would provide us with a believable reason for going to Germany. Here again, my survival instincts came into play. I reasoned that if questioned in Germany, it might be difficult to convince someone as to why we left Bendzin, which was not near the war zone, so I came up with the idea of using an address very near the battlefront, so we could claim that we were escaping the conflict. This story would be quite plausible and not easily checked; whereas, if our papers had a Bendzin address any German could simply pick up a phone, call the authorities in Bendzin, and discover that our papers were faked.

But where would we get still another set of false papers? I had a plan. I boarded an evening train to Jelesnia, intentionally arriving late at night. I made my way to the farm house where Father and I had stayed on our first trip to Jelesnia, and asked if they could rent me a room for the night, explaining that I couldn't find another place so late at night. They agreed to put me up for the night, and I went up to my room, but as soon as I was sure that they were all sound asleep, I crept downstairs to the living room. When I had stayed there before, I had noticed that the owner kept his important papers in a certain desk drawer. Opening this drawer, I found exactly what I had hoped to find. Among the documents in the drawer were the four identity papers for the residents of the house. "Borrowing" these papers, I slipped back upstairs, stuck the papers in the bottom of my briefcase, and went to bed. Having these papers was a matter of life and death for five members of my family, and I knew that the Poles could get them replaced by reporting that some scoundrel had stolen them.

My plan was, of course, to erase the farm family's names, and replace them with Jan Drzewo, Mieczyslaw Scrowronski, Jusek Fletzau, and Bronslowa Fletzau. These official credentials had the holders' fingerprints, but there was very little chance that anyone would check these. For a hometown I would use Nowogrodek, a small city near the Russian Front.

Following breakfast, I bought a few eggs from the farmer, which he carefully wrapped in newspaper to avoid breakage, and placed them in my briefcase. Feeling relieved that no one had discovered that their papers were missing, I walked to the station and caught the train to Katowice. As always, I killed time in Katowice until dark, and then took the train to Bendzin. As I descended the stairs from the platform in the Bendzin station, I was confronted by a pair of policeman, who were directing the incoming passengers to go to the right or to the left. I was sent to the left, which was not at all good, as this was the group who were detained for a brief questioning. Selecting out about a dozen people, including me, the police escorted my group to the police station for further interrogation.

Remembering the eggs in my briefcase, and knowing that it was illegal to possess them, I attempted to surreptitiously dispose of them as I was marching along behind the policemen. Unfortunately, as I was slowly lifting out the newspaper wrapped eggs, one of the officers spotted something white emerging from my briefcase, and stopped the group to investigate what I was up to. He asked me what I was trying to hide, so I sheepishly handed over the eggs. After confiscating the eggs, the officer, thinking that I might have more to hide, thrust his hand into the briefcase. My heart was pounding like a jackhammer, and had it been daylight he would have noticed that I had turned quite pale. After a few seconds, which seemed an eternity to me, his had came out, holding my original ID paper. After a brief examination of my ID, he handed the case back to me, allowing me to breathe again. Had the officer reached in another inch, and found the stolen ID papers, that would have been the end of my freedom, and most likely my life. It would also have scuttled the rest of the family's plans to get out of Poland.

But I wasn't out of the woods yet. When our little group arrived at the police station, and the interrogation began, the officer in charge said that I should be kept until the last. In no way did this smack of a good omen, but for some inexplicable reason, after all the others had been questioned, the officer simply told me that I was free to go. Perhaps, since it was late, the officer wanted to wrap things up and go home to a warm bed. Whatever the reason, I didn't waste any time in leaving. I knew that I had just dodged another bullet with my name on it.

It was now near midnight, and as I walked down the street, I seemed to be the only person out and about. The only one, that is, until I spied a pair of policemen headed in my direction. I was beginning to sweat when, just before they got to me, a streetcar rolled by, which I gratefully jumped aboard, and went back to the loft hiding place in Kamionka.

CHAPTER EIGHTEEN

Escape to Germany
(Told by Moishe/Mietek)

Finally, in mid November 1943, Father and I boarded the train in Katowice bound for Magdeburg. A key step toward the possible deliverance of the family was finally being taken. Father and I told the others that if we couldn't get word back to them within two weeks, then this meant we most likely would not be heard from again. The understanding was that the rest of the family should not attempt to follow us. We agreed to use a post office box in Dambrowa as a message drop. Because Jusek had once picked up mail in Bendzin when he worked at Mr. Krakowski's hardware store, which used box # 240, Jusek and I agreed that he should rent box # 240 at the Dambrowa post office, because it would be easy to remember the box number. Fortunately, that box was available and Jusek was able to rent it.

All went smoothly on the train trip, until we reached the station in Breslau, where we were faced with an unwelcome opportunity to test the believability of our fake ID papers. Two young Gestapo officers were going through our car, thoroughly scrutinizing every passenger's papers, and methodically closing in on two very nervous Jews. Then another minor miracle happened: Just before the officers got to Father and me, an air raid siren sounded, prompting the two Gestapo men to bolt for the exit and jump off the train, which immediately left the station. The rest of our journey was fairly uneventful, except for a delay of a couple of hours later that night, because Berlin was being pounded by Allied bombers, and our train couldn't enter the city.

Arriving at the Magdeburg station around midnight, I recommended that we get something to eat, suggesting that if we were arrested, at least we would have something in our stomachs. We got a bite to eat in the station café, and caught the train for Moeckern at about 3 am, without any problems. We disembarked in Moeckern with our luggage, and set off on foot Luehe. "Luggage" is a euphemism for a couple of banana crates, containing our meager possessions, tied up with stout string.

When we got to Luehe, we met a young boy, and we asked him to take us to the Bürgermeister's house. The boy led us there, and we found the Bürgermeister at home. It was our hope that this man could help us find work. One problem was that we had to pretend that we didn't speak or understand German, and the Bürgermeister didn't know any Polish; therefore, he didn't know what to do with us, except to call for the police in Moeckern. The police came over, and escorted us back to the police station in Moeckern. By now, it was late Friday afternoon, and all public offices were closed, so the police decided to hold us in the jail until Monday. The jailer put us in separate cells, but because it was very cold Father pleaded, through sign language, to let him sleep together with his comrade, for the sake of warmth. The jailer obliged, and even gave us a blanket. Later on, he brought us a big platter full of steaming potatoes, which we gobbled up with great relish. This was the first sizable meal for either of us in months.

By the next evening, being in jail and facing more interrogation was more than Father could handle. Once again, he became very depressed, and told me that he was going to hang himself. This was, of course, extremely upsetting for me, and I begged and pleaded with him to not do this terrible thing. I pointed out all the suffering we had already gone through, and had survived, and now it seemed that there was a real chance that we could possibly hold on until the end of the war. Also, it was obvious that if the police had any suspicion that we were Jews, they certainly wouldn't have given us food and a blanket. Further, I pointed out that if Father were to commit suicide, the Germans would reason that he must have had some cause for doing so, and would check me out more thoroughly, which would jeopardize the plan to rescue the rest of the family. My arguments were convincing enough that

Father abandoned the idea of suicide, and agreed to bear his anguish for the time being.

Father and I stayed in jail until Monday, where we were fed and treated fairly decently. That morning, Father was taken from our cell to the office, where he was told that he must pay 12 marks for our food and lodging in the jail. Father mimed that he had no money, but his friend had some; so they brought me to the office, collected the 12 marks, and put me back in my cell. About an hour later, I was taken back to the office again. In the office was a German, called Willy, and they indicated to me that I should go with him. I had no choice but to obey, and I also decided that Willy was probably OK because, although Germans did not normally shake hands with Poles, Willy did anyway. So even though I knew that my hand was too soft to be a worker's hand, it appeared that either Willy didn't notice or didn't want to notice, for which I was grateful. But when I returned to my cell to collect my few belongings, Father was no longer there, and I couldn't find out where they had sent him, and I had no way to look for him, so I followed Willy out of the station.

Willy rode off on his bicycle, signaling for me to follow him. I tried to keep up with him, carrying my clumsy box of belongings, but it was impossible. Willy finally realized that I was falling behind, so he slowed down to a normal walking pace. Together, we proceeded through Luehe, and on to Tryppehna, arriving at a farm owned by a German named Paul Stellar and his wife. I later learned that Willy was Frau Stellar's brother, who lived with them. Willy was somewhat mentally retarded, and therefore hadn't been taken into the Army.

By the time we arrived it was about 1:00 o'clock, so Frau Stellar gave me some lunch. I was the only one eating, and had the nervous feeling that everyone else was watching me while I ate, which was probably true, since I was gulping down my food like a starving man. Frau Stellar then took me to my room, which was over the stable. The room contained two beds, and was very clean, with fresh sheets on the beds. Cleanliness and neatness were things that I had almost forgotten about. After stowing my belongings, I went down to the stable, where Herr Stellar showed me two horses and a wagon that he expected me to harness and hitch up. I, of course, was a shoe salesman, not the farmer that I was pretending to be, and didn't have the least idea where to start or how to proceed. I started hooking things up in a very peculiar manner, while my boss stood by watching me with a mixture of amazement and disgust. Herr Stellar finally had enough, and pushing me aside, hitched up the team himself. I tried to explain in Polish that my way was the way they did it in Poland. Fortunately, Herr Stellar didn't understand Polish.

The two of us drove the team into the forest, where three of Stellar's workers were hard at work cutting down trees for firewood. They were all foreigners:

Ilyusha, who was to be my bunkmate, was a Ukrainian of about my age. Just before the German invasion of Russia, many of the young men in his hometown of Kiev, including Ilyusha, were shipped off beyond the Urals to work in the coal mines. Coal mining did not appeal to Ilyusha, who went AWOL, and made his way back to Kiev, where he was living when the German army occupied the city. The Germans were very short of farm labor, so he volunteered to be sent to Germany, where they found work for him on the Stellar's farm.

Felix was an older Pole, who had been working for the Stellars for about 20 years.

Malgoszka was a girl, about 19 or 20, who was of Ukrainian descent, but was born in eastern Poland. When the Germans occupied her hometown, she too volunteered for work in Germany, to escape the war zone.

I didn't realize until much later what a lucky hand Fate had dealt me. Only a week or so before Father and I had arrived at Moeckern, Paul Stellar had received orders to report to the Army. Although farmers were valuable to the Fatherland, the Russian campaign had taken such a toll on the army that draft boards were starting to scrape the bottom of the barrel. Before long they were calling up boys who were barely old enough to carry a rifle. Near the end of the war, they even drafted the simple Willy.

Because Paul Stellar would soon be leaving, I had been sent to his farm to provide additional manpower. Most of the farms were stocked totally with Polish refugees. Had I been sent to one of these farms, rather than one with a Ukrainian bunkmate, it would have been far more difficult—probably impossible—to pass myself off as a Pole for very long. My ending up with the Stellars in Tryppehna was yet another life-saving stroke of luck.

At first, I was given the task of loading the wood into the wagon, which was extremely hard for me, but I did my best, knowing how vital it was to keep this job. It was obvious to everyone that in my weakened condition, I wasn't capable of doing the work of a farmhand, but it was not unusual to find people in bad physical shape in these times, so they were understanding, and willing to give me time to build up my strength. At about five o'clock we drove the wagon, with a full load of wood, back to the farm. I now had to unload the wagon, which was doubly difficult because the branches hadn't been trimmed off.

By the time I had finished stacking the wood, I was totally exhausted, and as soon as I had finished my evening meal, I went straight to my room to collapse on the bed. To my surprise, Malgoszka soon showed up in the room, accompanied by her girl friend, Luszka, who was from Malgoszka's hometown, and had come to Germany with her. Luszka had reddened her lips and cheeks by rubbing wet red paper over them. Apparently she wanted to impress me, and was ready for a hot date. Malgoszka lay down next to Ilyusha, on his bed, and Luszka lay down next to me. Ilyusha was ready, willing and able to indulge in romance, but I had neither the strength nor the inclination. My mind was reeling with such problems as how to get a letter back to Jusek without arousing suspicion, or catching the attention of the authorities. My survival instincts told me that conversations with anyone should be kept to a bare minimum, and a romantic relationship would lead to more talking than would be prudent. I also knew that I didn't dare to expose the fact that I was circumcised. Luszka didn't give up on me so easily. She showed up the next night, and the third night, before deciding that there was something missing in my romantic makeup.

A few days after I arrived at the farm, two policemen came to the farm to check up on me. They were satisfied with my papers and my story, but informed me and my employer that I must get official local papers to work on the farm; so the next morning, Herr Stellar sent me to Loburg. I returned home that evening with not only the proper papers, but also a few cloth patches to sew on my clothes. These patches had a "P" on them, so now I was officially a Pole.

On my first Sunday on the farm, I was cheered up by a surprise visit from Father. I had, of course, been terribly concerned about where Father had been taken and if he was even still alive or not. The two of us decided to walk back to Moeckern, by way of Luehe. As we went past the Bürgermeister's house, he came running out, and for some unknown reason, commanded Father to go back to Moeckern, and me to go back to Tryppehna. Not wanting any trouble, we did as he ordered.

While wandering around, back in Tryppehna, I came upon a path leading out of the village. Having nothing better to do, I started walking along the path. To my surprise, after 3 to 4 of kilometers, I found myself in Moeckern. Walking around the town, I suddenly spied someone walking ahead of me, whom I immediately recognized as Father. Not wanting to frighten him, I walked closer to him, and softly spoke his name. We were now together again, in spite of the Bürgermeister. Father took me to see, from the outside, where he was living, and working at repairing shoes in a shoe store. The shop was run by a widow named Frau Bayer, who lived there with her 12-year-old daughter. They gave Father a place to sleep in the attic, along with a number of rats, mice, and spiders to keep him company. The Bayers, unaware that he understood German, often talked about him in his presence, referring to him as the "dumb Polack."

We next went to the café across from the train station for a bite to eat, and then to a bar for a beer. We sat at a table by ourselves, away from the local revelers, and ordered a couple of beers from the waiter. We sat sipping our beer, and talking, trying to be as inconspicuous as possible. After a while, a tall German walked over to our table, leaned over, placing his hands on the table between us, and in a low voice said, "I know who you are." Although this nearly paralyzed both of us with fear, we instinctively felt that our safest course of action was to pretend as though we had neither

seen nor heard him, and to continue to sip ou
he were not there. After a minute of silence, the n
and we never knew who he was, or if he really knew
us.

On the following weekend, I again took the path
to visit Father. We met, as agreed upon, in the café acrc   .et
from the station. Father complained to me that he wa: miserable
sleeping in the attic with all the rats and spiders. I felt that I had to
help him to find a more livable space. Being in a town where no
one knew me, I decided I could take a chance on speaking a little
German, so I asked Otto, the café owner, if he knew of a room that
my friend Jan could rent. Otto was delighted to hear this, as he
happened to have a room upstairs that he had been trying to rent
for some time. Upon inspecting the room, Jan and I were more
than pleased. It was clean and airy, with a washbasin, nightstand
and easy access to bathroom facilities. We wanted to pay Otto right
then and there, but Otto informed us that he must get permission from Jan's employer, Frau Bayer, and he must receive the rent
money from her. Getting Frau Bayer's consent proved to be no
problem; so Jan bade farewell to his verminous roommates in the
attic, and relocated to more wholesome surroundings.

Jan told me that he had not eaten an egg in a long time, and
maybe I, living on a farm, could get him one. So, before my next
visit, I sneaked out to the chicken house, and stole an egg from a
hen's nest, which I proudly presented to my father. Jan stared at
the egg, then back at me, and then asked disgustedly, "Is this your
idea of a joke?" I looked closely at the egg, and for the first time
saw that it was made of wood. I had robbed the nest of a wooden
decoy egg, which I didn't know was commonly put in a hen's nest
to encourage her to lay more eggs there. When I returned to the
farm, the first thing I did was to stealthily return the egg to the
nest. The next morning, a very puzzled Frau Stellar brought a
mystery story to the breakfast table. "A strange thing happened
overnight. When I checked one of the hens' nests yesterday, a
wooden egg I'd put there was missing, but when I looked this
morning, it's there again." Everyone, especially me, looked duly
mystified.

s and my very lives hinged upon our ability to convince all
ose in contact with us that we were Christians. To carry this off
was no small challenge for two orthodox Jews who had never even
set foot in a church, nor had much intimate contact with Christian
people. In addition, we were mostly surrounded by suspicious,
anti-Semitic neighbors. The first step was to start attending mass
every Sunday. On Jan's first entrance into the church he felt as
though God's wrath might send the building crashing down upon
his head, but his fear of being discovered as a Jew allowed him to
rationalize that the Lord would probably understand in light of
the special circumstances. The greatest danger was that he would
display his ignorance, and call attention to himself. All he could
really do was to watch the other parishioners, and mimic their actions. When they knelt, he knelt; when they crossed themselves,
he crossed himself, etc. In his own room, he decorated the walls
with numerous pictures of Christ, statues of Mary, and crucifixes.
Any visitor could easily see what a devout Christian he was. For the
next year and a half, until the end of the war, he was able to pull
off this charade.

Shortly after arriving in Tryppehna, I had managed to send
a letter back to Jusek at Box #240, Dambrowa Gornica, as prearranged. This letter contained my new address in Tryppehna, but
also, an admonition to not write to me. So, when I received a letter from Jusek, about three months later, I knew it must be very
urgent. The letter bore a postmark and a return address from
Heidelberg, Germany. I didn't find out how this postmark came to
be on the letter until after the war.

This Heidelberg postmark was the result of a series of adven-
tures that Father and I were completely unaware of. Not too long
after we left for Germany, the influx of Poles returning to Kamionka
made hiding above the stable much too risky, so Jusek and Mother
had little choice but to become permanent railroad nomads, living and sleeping on trains and in train stations. One of their trips
took them through Heidelberg. Jusek had written a letter to me,
asking for any last minute advice before he, Mother, and Poilka
came over to Magdeburg. When the train stopped in Heidelberg,

he asked the conductor how long they would be there. Learning that they had about five minutes, Jusek quickly wrote a fictitious Heidelberg return address on the envelope, jumped off the train, and popped it into a mailbox.

Poilka continued to work for the Unuckas while Jusek and Mother were living mostly on trains. They would purposely buy tickets that would give them plenty of time between trains so they could wash themselves and their clothes in the depot washroom. Mother detested her unsanitary condition, and even when they had little time between trains, Mother would go into the washroom, take off her dress and do her best to shake off the lice.

On one of these time-killing trips, their train stopped beside a group of pathetic looking Jewish slave laborers working on the track. Mother or Jusek would be putting their lives at risk to even speak to one of these poor starving wretches, but sometimes Mother's great heart overcame her instinct for self-preservation. Leaning out the window, she tossed a few pieces of her precious bread to the men. Jusek could not believe that she could do what he saw as a terribly foolish, risky thing, but he knew that Mother was Mother, and he couldn't change her.

They occasionally returned briefly to the stable in Kamionka. One day, walking on the street in Bendzin, Mother and Jusek noticed a great many people moving down the street as though all were headed to the same place. Curiosity drove them to investigate. What they came upon was a regular flea market, where the Poles were having a grand time pawing over and selling piles of the personal belongings that they had confiscated from the deported Jews. Mother later said that it tore the heart out of her breast to witness this ghoulish spectacle.

Their position, of living in limbo, became increasingly dangerous and difficult, until finally a series of events happened that made them realize some drastic change had to be made, and soon. Twice someone had recognized Mother, and called her by name. Terrified, she did the only thing she could do, which was to pretend she had not heard them, and walk away, with her legs on the verge of collapsing.

Jusek also had his frightening moments. A man once followed him down the street, calling after him, "I know who you are. You're Jusek Szpringer."

Jusek tried to ignore the man, but the man kept after him, until finally Jusek turned toward him and angrily snarled, "I don't know who you are, so leave me the hell alone."

But the man was not so easily deterred, and kept following him, and yelling at him, so Jusek just kept walking faster and faster, and turning corners, until he finally eluded him, and escaped what was a potentially disastrous situation. Perhaps the man meant him no harm, and only wanted to talk to him, but that was not a chance that Jusek could afford to take.

When I had written back to Jusek, I had warned him not to make the same mistake that Father and I had made. Our landing in jail could very well have spelled the end of us. I advised Jusek to avoid small town authorities, and go directly to the employment office in Magdeburg. Once he got my letter, Jusek immediately proceeded to prepare for the trip. First, he rounded up Poilka from Cieszyn. Then, using the technique that I had taught him, he altered the addresses on their ID papers, using Białystok as their hometown, since it was now just east of the front lines. Saying farewell to Bendzin, in March, 1944, Jusek, Poilka, and Mother boarded the train in Katowice, and headed for Magdeburg. Before picking up Poilka, Jusek had gone to Ludwigsdorf in an attempt to fashion an escape for Dora, but I will let her tell more about that later.

CHAPTER NINETEEN

Life as Poles in Hitler's Backyard
(Told by Laya/Poilka)

With renewed hope, Jusek, Mother, and I pulled into Magdeburg in March 1944. Following the advice in Mietek's second letter to Jusek, warning about the close call they had with the police in Moeckern, we went straight to the local employment office, not the police station. Using our usual caution, Jusek went into the office alone, while Mother and I stayed outside in the cold, praying that nobody would become suspicious of us and ask who we were. For all we knew, Jusek might not come out of the office once he went in, and we would be on our own in a strange land, but once again the Szpringer luck held.

After what seemed an eternity, Jusek finally did come out. He had had trouble because they couldn't understand Polish. They finally figured out that he was speaking Polish and found someone to translate. He told them he was from the farm, and that he could handle a team of horses and wagon. He also had a mother and sister who wanted to work. Workers being in great demand, we were immediately sent to work on a farm in Ottersleben, an area on the southwest outskirts of Magdeburg. The farm, owned by a German named Herr Boekelman, employed about thirty workers. "Employed" is a euphemism for taking advantage of desperate people, who were willing to do hard labor for a roof and slim food rations.

In the town, near Herr Boekelman's fields, the workers lived in barracks–one for men and one for women. Since we were the only family unit, our family was given a small hut for ourselves near the men's barracks. We had a small room with three beds, a table, a bench, and a stove. We had mattresses made out of feed sacks, filled with straw. The room was very cramped, so the table was set next to one of the beds, which was used in lieu of a chair. Luxury it wasn't, but it sure beat hiding in the loft in the Kamionka.

We Fletzaus had one serious problem–Mother spoke Polish with a decided Jewish accent, and looked more Semitic than Jusek and I. It would have been impossible for her to work day after day alongside the Polish workers, who were the major component of the labor force, without soon being recognized as a Jew. Therefore, as soon as we arrived at the farm, Jusek explained to the foreman that his mother was ill and could not work until she felt stronger. The foreman, Herr Schum, was a tall, gaunt, severe looking German of middle age. The black patch he wore over one eye, which he had lost in the First War, gave him an outright sinister aspect. But his appearance was somewhat misleading, as he really was not such a bad sort. He allowed Mother to be temporarily relieved of work duties.

While Jusek and I had the opportunity to go out and work, and maintain an active life, Mother only went out of the room at night to use the toilet, making sure first that no one else was there. If she had to go in the daytime she used a bucket in the room. This cramped little room was Mother's whole world for fourteen months. She spent her days pacing, for exercise, in the little space she had, or sewing and washing, or just sleeping. Of course this lifestyle really did have a debilitating effect on her physical and mental health. We could see that she was often very tired and in pain, but we knew that Mother was Mother and she would never let on that something was wrong with her. She didn't want to upset us. We did all we could to comfort her and cheer her, but how much could we do?

After a month or so, Herr Schum began asking Jusek when his mother would be able to work, pointing out that she was receiving a food ration for which she was doing no work. Jusek stalled him for some time with one excuse or another, but finally Herr Schum insisted that she be taken to a doctor for an examination. Jusek knew this would spell disaster, so he claimed she was too weak to move. Schum countered by telling him that a doctor would be sent to see her in a few days. Having a few days warning before the exam, Mother taped some coins and salt to her leg, which created a vile looking, nasty infection and causing a fever, which convinced the doctor that she was indeed not fit to work. Throughout the year and a half we stayed on the farm, various people tried to get Mother to come out, but through clever diversions Jusek succeeded in keeping Mother safe and completely out of sight.

The farm owners gave the workers no money, clothes or any other goods whatsoever, and only a subsistence level food ration. Jusek, Mother and I didn't just surrender to our deprived life, but continually made our life better by ingenuity—something that Jusek was a master at. Since I worked in the fields, I was able to high-grade part of each harvest for our dinner. In fall and summer we harvested potatoes, cabbages, and onions. In the late summer time we cut and threshed wheat. In the beginning I, being a city girl, suffered a lot during the wheat harvest. I had no shoes, and walking on the wheat stubble was like walking on a bed of nails. After a while I caught on to the knack of sliding my feet through the stubble rather than stepping down on it. Before long, skinny little me became a real farmhand. Although younger and not so strong as the other women, I pulled my own weight—whether pitching bundles of wheat onto wagons at harvest time, or following the plowman to pick up and sack potatoes. Jusek marveled at me, and told me, "I don't know how you do it. I, myself, couldn't keep up with you in the fields."

Jusek's talents as a jack-of-all-trades earned him special respect and favor from his bosses. He never had to work in the fields. Herr Boekelman once asked him, "How is it that you're so smart? When I tell you to do something, you learn it right away, and you even come up with your o\wn ideas to do the job better. The other Poles seem to have heads made of wood." Wisely, Jusek modestly tried to play down any difference between him and his "fellow Poles."

Early on, Jusek and I started going to the trash dump, where we salvaged some old banged-up pots and an old broken grinder, which Jusek repaired to working order. We could now grind up the corn that I had "requisitioned", and make cornmeal for cornbread. The farm stored its various freshly harvested crops in the barn. Once the food dried out, it was ready to transport away. So I would use this opportunity to steal corn, peas, or whatever I could fill my sweater with. I would tell the boss at night that I had forgotten my sweater in the barn and then go in and fill it up with food. I always managed to pilfer a little of whatever we were harvesting, to supplement the stingy food rations doled out by the owners.

At the end of the work day harvesting cabbages, I got the bright idea to smuggle one of them home by cutting it in half and inserting the two halves in my blouse. I was a properly brought up and very naïve young girl, and didn't yet realize how much attention men give to these matters. As I left the field, Herr Schum's one good eye opened wide, and he exclaimed, "Poilka! What's going on here? You went into the field this morning flat-chested, and now look at you! Give me the damned cabbage, you little thief!" But he was not totally successful in restraining a smile, which almost spoiled his stern image.

The Boekelman farm had some workers from the Ukraine and Russia, but they were mostly Poles. The Russians weren't too bad to work with, but the Ukrainians and Poles were really unpleasant. They were uncooperative, lazy, and hard to get along with even in the most trivial matters–plus they were suspicious. They continually picked on me, and worst of all, often accused me of looking and acting like a Jew. Every time I was teased about looking like a Jew, a pang of fear shot through me. My only defense was to pretend to ignore them. I felt that my nose was largely to blame, as it tended to point downward rather than skyward, as did most of the Poles' noses. The solution, I reckoned, was to train my nose upward. This I did by sleeping every night with a handkerchief tied under my nose, and up over the top of my head, tight enough to apply upward pressure. Although performing this nose elevation ritual for more than a year produced no discernable physical effect, it did serve a positive psychological purpose. All aspects of my life were a collection of outside forces acting on me, with no control on my part. Attempting to alter my nose gave me a feeling that I was in control of something. Looking back, we can all laugh about it, but at the time, it was no joke. I was genuinely in fear for my life, and justifiably so.

There was also a small group of POWs from Yugoslavia on the farm. These POWs received an occasional package of food and personal items through the Red Cross. Jusek would manage to do a favor for one of these POWs, and in return receive some item that made our life more tolerable, such as a bar of soap. A little soap doesn't sound like a big deal, unless you don't have any.

From time to time, Jusek would do some favors for the kitchen staff, and they in turn would slip him a few food coupons. This enabled me to go into the village and buy a little extra food. We couldn't afford meat, but the butcher would sell me his extra bones, which Mother threw into the soup. Occasionally we would get a piece of meat from some poor old horse who could no longer pull his load. He had met the same fate as the old and sick Jews whom the Nazis had culled out, and sent to the gas chambers. Although Mother would cook the horsemeat for her children, she could not force herself to eat meat from a horse. It just simply would not go down her throat.

In order to keep up appearances I had to go to church, just like Jan and Mietek. Today I joke that maybe I'm alive now because I had two Gods. Like her husband, Mother had a picture of Mary hanging over her bed. Mother often said later that she thought maybe Mary had looked after her; after all, Mary was a Jew too. Like my father, when I went to church I didn't have the least idea as to what to say or do so I just watched the others and did as they did. Seeing all the others going into this little booth, I figured that I should do likewise. I didn't know it was the confessional both; I didn't even know what confession was. I sat down in the booth, the little window opened and I just sat there, my heart pounding with fear, not knowing what to do next. I hadn't expected someone to be on the other side. After a minute or so of silence the little window closed, and I went out. I knew that somehow I hadn't done what I was expected to do, so the next Sunday I went into the booth and when the little window opened, I sat trembling with panic for a few seconds, then I started mumbling something in Polish. The Priest, not understanding a word I said, gave up and closed the window, and I went home. After that, I decided that it might be best to just avoid confession. As with my attempts at nose lifting, I laugh about it now, but it was no laughing matter then.

By 1945 the area around Ottersleben, including the farm, came into the sphere of Allied bombing—the Americans by day and the British by night. In spite of the danger, we were thrilled at the sight and sound of the bombers—surely the end of the war must be near. More and more bombs were falling in the Magdeburg area, as the Allies started to bring the war home to Germany. Fighter planes strafed the fields where I was working, killing some of the workers. Jusek helped in the construction of air-raid shelters, which were of course intended exclusively for use by the Germans. However, when the siren blew in the middle of the night, my family and a few others jumped out of bed and ran into the shelter. We weren't supposed to be there, but no one told us that we had to leave. Rather than risking being blown to bits in our little room, Mother covered her Semitic face with her shawl and ran to the shelter with us.

One night a bomb exploded very close to the women's barrack, creating a gigantic crater and destroying a large section of the tile roof. Some of the farmhands, including me, were put to work repairing the roof. Since I was the smallest and lightest, the group decided I was the logical one to crawl around on the damaged rafters to replace the missing tiles. One of the older Polish women, who took particular delight in tormenting me, demanded that I climb up the ladder onto the roof. The roof was very steep, and I was afraid to go up, but I was even more afraid of this woman. As my trembling legs slowly lifted me up the ladder, out of pure meanness, this nasty woman took hold of the ladder and shook it, giving herself and the other women a good laugh. When I came home in tears, Jusek decided we had had enough of this nonsense. He went out and called the woman over to him, lowering the boom on her in these explicit terms, "Now listen, you ugly bitch. If you don't leave Poilka alone, I'll break your ugly neck!" This was the last time this woman gave me any trouble.

CHAPTER TWENTY

More Trouble for Mietek
(Told by Moishe/Mietek)

Over on the Tryppehna farm, I was having problems of my own. I found that in addition to having no farming skills, I was not able to handle the work physically. I was just too weak. After about five days of difficult work with horses and plowing, Stellar's workers moved to the relatively easier job of threshing wheat, which was a great relief to me, as I was just about to the point where I was sure that I couldn't handle the work any longer. The wheat threshing was not only a little easier, but it required no particular skill as well. I simply took a pitchfork and tossed the wheat to another man who in turn fed the threshing machine. I did my best to stay away from any job that required any knowledge of farm skills. As soon as I had to work with any animal or farm machine, I was stumped, but I was eager to learn—my life depended on it.

Frightening little incidents often cropped up unexpectedly. For instance, one weekend before leaving to visit Jan, I asked Malgoszka to feed the cow for me. She replied, "You say 'krowa' (cow) like a Jew."

Careful as I was, I couldn't be completely on guard every minute of the day. I did have a few dangerously careless lapses. After I had been there for several months I became a little more relaxed and a few times lowered my shield. For example: A pretty young German girl of about nineteen, wearing a Hitler Youth uniform, was visiting the farm. One morning she and I were picking grapes together. Being smitten by her charms, I lost control of my good senses, and couldn't resist the temptation to chat with her in German. Later on, when I returned to the house, Frau Stellar remarked, "Mietek, Ursula said you were talking to her in German."

I didn't respond, but just walked out of the house saying to myself,
"Mietek, what kind of a goddamned fool are you?   If you're not
more careful, you'll end up in a cattle car."

But often enough, I did make good decisions that worked for
me and kept my disguise working. I realized that it must look peculiar to others that I sat around in my room every evening, and
didn't socialize with anyone, and that my solitary behavior might
draw suspicion. So I started going to the village gasthaus in the
evening for a beer, and when I got back, I would tell Ilyusha that I
had been talking to this or that Pole. I did, in fact wish to ingratiate myself with a certain Pole- a very large former soldier named
Kazhik. I got a pair of half-soles and some cobbler's nails from Jan
– very valuable items in these times. I presented these to Kazhik,
and while we were having a beer together, I told him how Ilyusha
was always making fun of me because I was a Pole, and joking about
how we Poles had lost the war in only three weeks. Kazhik looked
up Ilyusha, and served him notice that, "If you don't like Poles,
you can deal with me, not Mietek."

The next time he saw me, an obviously subdued Ilyusha asked
me, "Why did you tell Kazhik what I said about the Poles?"

As I had hoped, the huge Pole had made a big impression, and
Ilyusha was noticeably nicer to me after that.

Although I finally settled into my job on the farm, and appeared to be accepted, I was always under scrutiny, and was the
subject of chronic suspicion. Incidents highlighting this mistrust
surfaced all too often. For instance, once while we were working
in the field together, Willy asked me, "Are you really a Pole? All
the other Poles drink a lot and use bad language all the time, but
you're not like that."

I replied that I was indeed a Pole, and there were many other
Poles just like me back home. Willy, being not too bright, was easily convinced, but not everyone was like Willy.

One weekend afternoon, Ilyusha, whose bed was by the window, had three of his Russian buddies in his room, just relax-
ing and telling stories, when I came in and lay down on my bed
by the door. After a short while, Ilyusha and friends decided to
go out. I pretended to be sleeping, and as they passed my bed,

Ilyusha suggested, "Let's take down Mietek's pants and see if he's circumcised".

Two of the others were ready to have some fun at my expense, but the third, a tall man with an air of leadership, stopped them by saying, "Leave him alone. He wants to live just like the rest of us."

After they exited the room, I, who had been feigning sleep through the whole incident, felt a deep gratitude toward this tall Russian for quite likely having just saved my life. I wished there were some way to thank him, but, of course, this was impossible.

One evening Ilyusha, who was an educated man with a university degree, very proudly told me about how, when he was in Kiev, he had discovered a Jew and turned him in to the Nazis. All I could do was to pretend not to be interested.

Another day, after spending many hours shocking wheat in the field, Ilyusha and I were hot, sweaty, and itching from the chaff that had worked its way under our clothes. Ilyusha said, "Come on Mietek, let's go down and wash up."

This may have sounded innocent enough, but my survival instincts told me that Ilyusha's real motive was to check me out in the nude, to see if I was circumcised. So I came up with some excuse to wash myself later.

One time I was sweeping the porch with a corn broom, when Ilyusha came walking by. He stopped and stood watching me, hands on hips, and after a minute remarked, "You know Mietek, you sweep like a Jew!"

When Poles swept, they used long forceful strokes, not like my short, careful motions. Another time Ilyusha told me that I walked like a Jew.

Ilyusha often tried to drag me into discussions of politics, but I kept it as a firm survival rule that my only three safe topics of discussion were work, weather, and food.

The preceding incidents are just a few examples of how precarious of my life was, and the constant pressure under which I lived. Sometimes the stress was too much, and I would go off by myself, and when I was sure that no one could hear me, I would sit by a hedgerow, and with tears of despair escaping from my eyes,

I'd revive my will to live by softly singing "Hatikvah," the Zionist anthem, which became the Israeli national anthem.

Like Poilka, I too spent many hours in my room trying to pull my nose upward, so it would look more like a Polish nose and less like a Jewish nose, but I was no more successful than Poilka.

Noticing my regular Sunday outings, Frau Stellar would ask me if I was going to visit my girlfriend. With a laugh that only I could fully appreciate, I always replied that yes, I was going to see my girlfriend. Years later, Father liked to laugh about being my "girlfriend" during our time in Tryppehna and Moeckern.

In June of 1944 a Pole came up to me and said "You have survived." I didn't respond, and the man walked away without further explanation, leaving me deeply troubled that this fellow might have seen through my disguise.

The hidden life also required great forbearance at times. For instance, one day some people were speculating about whether or not all of the Jews were dead. One of the other men said that "Hitler doesn't like the Jews because they are too smart."

Knowing that many people felt this way, I always made a conscious effort to not appear to be too smart myself. But then too, I didn't want it to appear that I was avoiding all discussions. It was a constant and delicate balancing act, in which the slightest misstep by me could draw unwanted attention and suspicion to myself.

Taking a break from work one day, I was sitting in the shade with a group of Poles. One of them had lived in a town by the river Bug, which at this point marked the border between Germany and Russia before the German invasion of Russia. Great numbers of fleeing Jews came to this Pole's town, seeking a means to cross the River Bug, to escape into Russia. This man was bragging and laughing about how he would take money from the Jews, row them out to deep water, tip the boat over, and swim back to his dock, pulling his boat by a rope. It was his belief that the Jews, who were fully clothed, and did not know how to swim, had all drowned. He made a nice profit for himself, perpetrating this trick several times a night. The anti-Semitic Poles all roared with laughter at this story, and I had no choice but to sit there and listen to this horrible account, and force myself to laugh along with them.

A woman in her thirties, named Hilda, lived with her teenage daughter upstairs in the Stellars' house. She paid for her keep by helping Frau Stellar with the laundry, and other chores, as needed. On weekends, Hilda would doll herself up in sexy clothes and heavy makeup, and go into Magdeburg. It was generally assumed that she was working as a lady of the night. Across the road Greta, a woman from Hamburg, was living in a small house with her two small children. Allied bombing had destroyed her home, and she had sought out the farm as a refuge.

Greta and Hilda were thinning carrots in the field across the road from the farmhouse, all the while chatting with each other. I was standing nearby tending to a pair of horses, but close enough to follow their conversation. Hilda was telling her that she didn't like the fact that her daughter had started staying out late, sometimes coming home after midnight. Greta strongly advised Hilda to put a stop to this right away, and take a belt to the girl, but Hilda shrugged her shoulders, and replied with a chuckle, "The cow forgets that she was once a calf."

Greta looked over in my direction, and said to Hilda that she was sure that I understood every word they were saying. At this, Hilda walked over behind a haystack, and beckoned me to come over to her. When we were together, Hilda told me to take my pants down, but I only shook my head and pretended that I didn't understand, and walked away. The two women got a big laugh out of this.

As the battlefront moved closer, increasing numbers of refugees passed through the farm, mostly at night. Some were Jews from concentration camps, where the guards had fled the approaching Russians, and some were escapees from death marches. The Germans caught many of these unfortunate souls who, after years of torment, were on the very edge of freedom, and shot them on the spot. It was during this time that two Jewish girls, who were obviously escapees, were standing close to me and were talking in Yiddish, apparently thinking that no one would understand them. Of course this was a very foolish thing for them to do, and I wanted to warn them to be more careful, but I knew that I had to pretend that I didn't know what they were saying. Herr Stellar said to me "Mietek, you don't know what they are talking about, do you?"

Of course I couldn't tell my boss that I knew exactly what they were saying any more than I could tell the girls themselves that I was Jewish too. I felt bad about it, but I just had to let them go on without warning them.

A Polish girl, who was fleeing the advancing front, ran into Ilyusha and me while we were working in the field. Knowing that she must be hungry, Ilyusha gave her a part of his sandwich. She proceeded to tell us that we would soon see many others like her, who would be fleeing from the battle front. She then advised us that if we saw someone with a number tattooed on his arm, we should know he was a Jew. The obvious implication being that we would know not to help him. I took the horses and quietly moved away, burning under the collar, but I was at least glad that I was not the one who had given her part of my sandwich.

An older Jewish woman and three teenage girls, all from Łodz, who had escaped from a death march, found the farm at night, and hid in the bomb shelter. Malgoszka discovered them in the morning, and told me that there were some Poles in the bomb shelter. I went over and talked to them, and immediately recognized them as Jews, so I asked Malgoszka to give them some potatoes, which she did, not knowing that they were Jews. I then went to the Bürgermeister of Tryppehna, and obtained four patches with a "P" on them, and gave them to the women to sew on their clothes. I advised them to separate, and move on. I have no idea what became of them.

Although Ottersleben and Tryppehna were only about 25km apart, contact between the two parts of our family was non-existent. Naturally, there was a great yearning in both camps to learn how the others were getting along. Neither one even know if the others were still alive. Jusek, being always the adventurous one, decided that regardless of the great risk, he had to try to make contact with his father and me. One Sunday in May 1944, when I arrived on my weekly visit to Jan, it was plain to see that he was much more upbeat than usual. As soon as we were alone in his room, Jan came out with "Guess who came to see me yesterday?"

I wasn't interested in playing guessing games. I practically demanded of Father, "Tell me, who?"

With a proud twinkle in his eye, Jan announced, "Yossel!" I was speechless for a few seconds, but then began bombarding him with questions:

"Are Mother and Laya okay?" "Where are they?" "Does he know anything about Dora?"

I was so thrilled and excited that I could hardly contain myself. I get all choked up when I'm reminded of that moment, and I always will, to the end of my days, After answering all of my questions that he could, he told me that Jusek had promised to try to come again next Saturday. Although Jusek did return to visit Father two more times, I never had a chance to see him in Moeckern. Jan and I then drank a toast to the Family, and feeling more optimistic than I had in a very long time, I headed back to the Stellar farm. I was aware, of course, that anything could still happen, but I also knew that getting the family safely out of Poland and into Germany was the best thing we could have done, and was a giant leap on our pathway to survival. As I was striding along, I realized that I had a smile on my face. I had better regain control of my emotions before I got back to the farm, or I might attract a lot of unwanted questions.

CHAPTER TWENTY ONE

"L'chayim!"
(Mietek continues)

As 1944 turned into 1945, there were many obvious signs that Germany was going to lose the war. But since all the German news sources were controlled by the government, all the German people heard was about their glorious victories—unless they were illegally listening to BBC. I even heard Hitler on the radio talking about the V-1 and V-2 rockets, and how the Germans would destroy England and win the war. But the turn of the tide of war began to give me a feeling of confidence. I started visiting Father more often—about twice a week.

This new confidence was a bit premature and almost got me into serious trouble. I had become disgruntled over the fact that the Stellars were still eating better than I was, dining on ham, while they were only feeding me cheese. While grousing about this with one of the other workers, the two of us agreed to go on strike for better food. But Frau Stellar gave us a swift reality check–if we didn't want to work she would call the police to take us away. How big a fool could I be? I should have been happy that I was still alive. But perhaps, in a perverse way, this stupid stunt might have helped to convince them that I was not a Jew; surely, no Jew in hiding could possibly do such a moronic thing.

On both sides of the Elbe, rumors were increasingly flying about, that the Americans and the Russians were getting closer, the war would soon end, and the day of salvation was at hand. Liberation by anyone was, of course, the dream of all the refugees, but given a choice they would much prefer it be by the Americans rather than the Russians, who were known to often brutalize the victims as well as the perpetrators, especially the women. What the people were unaware of was that the western Allies and the Russians had reached an agreement to the effect that the Elbe River was to be the dividing line between their respective areas of control, with their respective armies stopping at the Elbe. Since the Elbe runs through eastern Magdeburg, it was inevitable that the Fletzaus would be liberated by the Americans, while Jan and I would be freed by the Russians.

To the east of the Elbe, where Father and I were, there was more and more evidence that the Russians were indeed approaching, and the end of the war was in sight. I started visiting Jan whenever I wanted to. On the way to Moeckern, one evening after work, I spotted a young man standing by an abandoned barn. The man, an Italian in an Italian army uniform, asked me if I had any food. I said that I couldn't help him, and went on to meet Father. On my way back, I stopped at the barn, where the Italian and a tall, thin, but attractive young woman were sitting by the door. I sat down with them, and joined them in a cautious conversation. The girl, Rivka, was from Vilna, and had escaped from a death march after the Stutthof concentration camp in Danzig was evacuated. More than half of the prisoners who started this death march died during the march.

She asked me, "People usually think I'm Italian, what do you think I am?"

I was sitting cross-legged on the ground, and made the sign of a star on my knee. Rivka asked, "Five points?"

Which would indicate Russian, but I said, "No, six."

Meaning, of course, Jewish. Her eyes opened large, and she came up very close to me and asked, earnestly, "Are you Jewish?"

Oh, how I was aching to tell her that I was, but I hadn't survived all these perilous years by being incautious, so I shook my head, "No".

These were desperate times, and had I told her the truth, this otherwise nice young woman, or her friends, might have used this knowledge to blackmail me for food, or who knows what else.

Rivka told me the story of how, while in Stutthof, she had been selected to go to the gas chamber, but had successfully bribed one of the guards with some gold pieces, and that was why she was still alive. This was the first time I had heard about the gas chamber at Stutthof. The next time I went to the barn, there was a second Jewish girl there, also from Vilna and Stutthof. She had been too afraid to come out before. By now I was becoming more at ease with and trusting of this group, so I finally confided in them that I too was indeed a Jew.

On a subsequent visit to Moeckern, Jan told me of two more Jewish girls who had come to the shoe shop when he was alone there, and had asked for food. He found them a piece of bread, and ask them to come up to his room. He could see that they were very leery of this idea, so he said to them, "Look, I'm an old man. What could I do to you?"

Their fears somewhat assuaged, they followed him to his room. To this point the girls had no idea that he was Jewish, or that he knew that they were, so they were quite taken aback when he poured a little whiskey all around, raised his glass, and toasted "L'chayim!," ("To Life!"). The girls must have been stunned to hear him speak Hebrew, but joined him in the toast, and after a short visit, during which Jan suggested a place they might hide, they parted company.

When Father recounted this little story to me, I was absolutely livid. I could not believe my ears. I let father know how I felt with something to this effect:

"Are you out of your mind?! Here we have survived the Nazi occupation, the Ghetto, Judenrein, and all the rest, and now, when the war is almost over, you put our lives at risk so that you can enjoy a round of drinks with a couple of pretty girls!"

Father sat silent for a minute, and finally said, "You know, they were very nice girls. I would really like to arrange for you to marry one of them."

How could this not soften me up a bit? But I wasn't ready to even dream about marriage in these insane times.

Under normal circumstances, the farm workers reported to work at about 6 a.m., but one morning after breakfast, Paul Stellar's brother told all the farm workers not to go to the field, but to follow him into the village. In the village, we were put to work building anti-tank barricades out of railroad ties. While we were working, an old man, from a nearby village, came by pulling a handcart. He told us that the Russians were already in his village. Not long after that, a car pulled up, and out stepped a Russian officer. His aide proceeded to pass out a leaflet signed by Marshal Georgy Zhukov. We were informed that we should go about our normal life, and no harm would come to us. My liberation had come so undramatically that it was hard for me to grasp that I had been freed, but when Ilyusha came over and told me to go back to the farm and feed the horses, I just looked at him, and said, "If you want the horses fed, go feed them yourself." I was finished with taking orders.

I was eager to get to Moeckern and tell Father the good news, but first I went to Frau Stellar, and speaking German to her for the first time, demanded to have my ID papers that the Stellars had been holding. I retrieved both my employment forms and the papers I had stolen from the farmer in Jelesnia and had modified. Frau Stellar now realized that the shoe was on the other foot and she needed to curry favor with me, so she told me that she owed me a half a year's back pay. I knew this, but had been afraid to complain about it earlier. Even when I was being paid, I had only received 17 marks per month. I told her, "Keep your money. Why do I need money–I have life." I then showed her that I had plenty of money hidden in various compartments in my jacket. Shaking her head, Frau Stellar asked me, "Who are you"?

I told her, "Someday I will let you know."

I then hurried over to Moeckern. When I found Father, I was startled to find that the Russian tanks had already rolled into Moeckern the day before. Prior to their entry, the Russians had dropped leaflets saying that civilians should fly white flags so as to be left alone by the advancing Russian troops. Father felt safe enough to go openly to city hall and to ask for a white flag.

One tank had driven to the city hall, and the tank commander ordered the Germans to hoist a white flag over the building. When Father went out on the street, there were no Germans to be seen – only Russians. To the Russians, the conquering of the little town of Moeckern called for a celebration—The Russians needed little excuse to raise a few glasses of vodka. A large group of soldiers, standing beside a tank, spotted Father, and called him over. When they discovered that he understood Russian, they were quite surprised and somewhat suspicious, but they ordered him to lead them to the nearest gasthaus.

Inside the gasthaus, Father was ordered to tell the owner to take out every bottle of liquor that he had, and place it on the bar, so the soldiers could help themselves, and then told him to join them. In a small group talking with the commandant, Father spotted a Russian officer who looked to him to be Jewish. He walked over to him, raised his glass, and said, "L'chayim". The officer looked quite surprised, and asked him why he had said "L'chayim" to him. Father answered, "Because I am Jewish, and if I'm not mistaken you are, too."

The officer was incredulous. He stared at my father, and in a serious tone, said "Do you know that we have come all across Russia, Poland, and half way into Germany, and the whole way, not one Jew have we seen? Now you walk up to me, and tell me that you are a Jew, and you expect me to believe you. You'll have to prove it."

Whereupon, Father dropped his pants to show that he was circumcised, but the officer wasn't convinced. He said that lots of people besides Jews were circumcised. This was exceedingly ironic, as the Germans never hesitated to accept this test as proof of a man's being Jewish.

The officer began quizzing him with detailed questions on Jewish ritual, such as:

"What do you wear when you go into a synagogue?" "What does the blue thread in the Tallis mean?" "If you are Jewish, then tell me when you get up in the morning, what do you say? What kind of prayer?" "On which arm do you put on the tefillin?"

Father readily answered all these questions, and the Russian was finally convinced.

Slapping Father on the back, the officer told Father that he could go into any store he chose, and help himself to whatever he needed. His first choice was to go into a clothing store and pick out something decent to wear, and then he went to Frau Bayer's place. He walked in and began speaking to her in German, which caught her completely by surprise. She stammered out, "Jan, since when do you speak German?"

His reply was, "The whole time I've been here I knew German and I understood everything you said about me. Do you know who you've had working for you? I'm a Jew."

She fainted.

Although we were indeed free, and had little to fear from the Germans, it took us a good many days to feel comfortable in shedding our disguises as Polish gentiles and to become our real selves. Well trained habits and behavior ingrained into our minds as a matter of life and death for almost two years couldn't be shed instantly, but after a while we allowed ourselves to say goodbye to Jan and Mietek, thanking them for all their help, and to welcome back Abraham and Moishe. "L'chayim." However, Jan and Mietek hung around with us for the rest of our lives.

Within a few days of liberation, the Russians put out a notice that all foreigners must go to the city of Cottbus, roughly 200 kilometers to the east, where they must register before they would be allowed to leave Germany for their respective home countries. I "organized" a wagon and two horses to take Father and me to the registration. One of these horses was young and strong, but the other was a candidate for the glue factory. We had only gone a few miles when we came upon the ruins of a German tank by the side of the road. My natural curiosity impelled me to look inside, and much to my delight I found an abandoned pistol. When I took this gun into my hand, something that I had never done before in my life, as if by magic, a feeling of great empowerment swept over me. Suddenly I had unlimited power. Nobody could touch me. I was the King of the World. I had never had such a feeling before. Now I had some sense of what it was that allowed the Nazis to act with such bravado. Of course, when I came back down to Earth, I realized that it was best not to be caught with this weapon, so I quickly secreted it among my belongings on the wagon.

A little further along into our journey, we were halted by a group of Russian soldiers, who demanded an explanation as to who we were and where we were going. The Russians were very skeptical of our explanation, that we were Jews attempting to return to our home in Poland. If we were Jews, why did we have hair? All of the other Jews who were on the road had shaven heads. The soldiers then turned their attention to the horses. In anticipation of just such an encounter, I had wrapped a rag around the leg of the healthy horse, and in response to the Russian's inquiry as to health of the animal, I lamented that it was in pathetic shape, and I was worried that it would never make it to Cottbus. The sergeant in charge of the group mounted the beast, to test this diagnosis, whereupon the horse began to jump and buck, throwing its rider to the ground. The soldier dusted himself off while yelling curses at me, and drawing his pistol. I said some silent prayers, being certain that, after all I had survived, I was now going to my grave over a stupid horse. Why he didn't shoot me I don't know. The Russian then asked me if I had any weapons, which I denied. Having learned not to take this man's word for anything, the sergeant ordered his men to search both of us and our wagon, and, of course, discovered my precious pistol. Much to my father and my chagrin the soldiers confiscated our healthy horse and my pistol, but at least we were still alive. The poor old plug was left to pull the wagon by himself, which he valiantly did, but his passengers had to get off and walk when we ascended any steep grades. After the completion of the eventful, but successful, journey to Cottbus, Father and I were now free to board a train back to Bendzin.

CHAPTER TWENTY TWO

American Saviors
(Told by Laya/Poilka)

Being cut off from schooling at the age of ten, and having read almost nothing in the following six years, I knew almost nothing about anything outside my own immediate surroundings. More and more I heard people talking about "the Americans" in such an exalted manner, but I had little concept of what an American was. I finally asked my mother, "Everybody keeps talking about, 'the Americans', 'the Americans.' Who are these Americans? Are they some kind of Gods or something?"

I was about to find out. We had, of course, no way of knowing that Father and Moishe had already been liberated, while on the Boekelman farm, Jusek, Mother, and I would have to wait a little longer for our freedom. The war finally landed firmly on our doorstep when the German army blockaded the streets and set up tank barriers. No one could go to work; there was nothing to do but stay inside and pray that you didn't become a battle casualty. Most of the German civilians fled, and before long, so did the German army. Then came that most glorious, wonderful moment of my life–into Ottersleben rumbled a huge olive drab machine with a white star on it, and from it emerged the long prayed for Americans. The three of us were too overcome with emotion to know how to react. Our hearts were overflowing with joy and relief, but our minds were almost afraid to accept what our eyes revealed. Was this real, or were we dreaming? We ran outside to stand, and stare, and weep. More than sixty years later I'm still brought to tears when I speak of that moment.

Although most of the Germans had run away, the soldiers told everyone left to stay where they were, as there was still fighting

going on all around, which was confirmed by the ongoing explosions and crackling of small arms fire. From many of the German
houses diehard civilians were shooting at the Americans–even
women, old men, and children were shooting, trying to protect
the Fatherland. After a couple of days the Americans gave the foreign workers the green light to move about freely, and even told
us to go into the town and help ourselves to whatever we needed;
which we all did with a vengeance.

We Szpringers (until this day, the Fletzaus) had very successfully trained ourselves not only to pass as Poles, but feel that we were
Poles. We were self-trained to suppress anything about ourselves
that was Jewish. These habits, and the constant fear of discovery,
developed over years, and etched into our minds, didn't just disappear as though a switch were thrown, simply because we were told
that we were free and safe. As with Moishe and Father, although
we were in fact out of danger, it took some time for the three of
us to come to grips with the reality of freedom, and to feel safe in
revealing our true identity as Jews.

As a case in point, Yossel spent much of the next few days scouting about the region hoping to find another Jew. After considerable
searching, he encountered a young man whom he thought looked
Jewish. Striking up a conversation with this fellow, he learned that
his name was Jacob Kupferberg. Jacob was from Poland, and he
had just been freed from a concentration camp near Magdeburg.
The two walked along, talking in Polish, until Yossel felt comfortable to confide in him, "You know, I'm Jewish, too." Jacob, taken
aback, and a little skeptical, replied,

"If you are really Jewish, why don't you speak to me in
Yiddish?"

Yossel opened his mouth, but no sound came out. He had very
successfully programmed his mind to equate speaking Yiddish
with the threat of death. It took him a minute or so of struggle to
overcome this training, and to allow any Yiddish words to escape.

Yossel took Jacob home with him to meet the family. When he
introduced him to Mother as a Jew, she broke into tears. She said
that he was the first Jew she had met, or even heard of, since the
war ended. She had begun to believe that her little family were the

only Jews left alive in Europe. For his part, when he was told that our family had survived the war without being caught and sent to a camp, Jacob could only sit and shake his head in disbelief. A whole family surviving Judenrein, and hiding out for almost two years! And in Germany! Could such a thing be possible?

Increasingly, we began to realize that our survival was not only possible, but it was a fact. It would take years though for us to fully come to terms with it.

When Mother finally accepted the reality of her freedom, she began venting her anger for her years of suffering and the knowledge of what the Germans had done. She didn't engage in violence, for that was completely foreign to her nature and upbringing. Instead, she began to confront every German she met, and, pulling no punches, proceeded to give them a vigorous lecture on the atrocities the Germans had committed against her people. This went on for weeks, until we became uncomfortable about her aggressive actions, and begged her to pull back a little. She finally relented when she realized that she wasn't generating any great feelings of guilt on the part of the Germans, and was only increasing her own frustration.

Yossel had an old address for Frau Schultz in Magdeburg, so he went into the city to find her. He had no way of knowing if she was at this address, or if she were even in Magdeburg. He found that her house had been destroyed by the Allied bombing, but by asking around he was able to locate her. By this time we had moved from the farm to a house in Ottersleben, so Yossel invited her, and her husband, who had returned from the army, to stay with him and his family. She gratefully accepted, and the Schultzes stayed with Yossel, Mother, and me for several weeks, until we were able to return to Bendzin. After a week or so, Theo showed up, and also moved in with us.

After re-establishing contact with Theo, following our escape from the Kamionka, Mother would sometimes slip over to his home after dark, to wash herself and her clothes. On the last of these visits, she realized that she had left a dress in his place with some gold coins hidden in one of the seams. Now that we were re-united, she asked him about the coins. He said that he knew nothing about any gold coins, but that when he got back to his family home in Trzebin, he would look for them and return them to us, if he could recover them. Eventually, Theo went back to Poland on the same train that we did, but when we got off at Bendzin, he went on to Trzebin. After he left on that train, none of our family ever saw him again. Years later, Yossel went back to Poland and looked for him, but with no luck.

CHAPTER TWENTY THREE

My Own War
(Dora's story)

So that is how the rest of my family managed to survive. But I haven't told you what was happening to me during all this time. To do so, I must now go back to late 1942, when I had just ransomed Mother out of the Nazi's clutches by turning myself in to the Germans.

Pulling into Auschwitz, the doors of all the cars were flung open. Waiting outside were SS men with clubs and rifles, and some of them holding back vicious dogs on taut leashes. Both clubs and dogs were liberally used to hurry the prisoners along. The people from all of the boxcars except mine were prodded into lines, and brought up before a Nazi doctor who looked them over and decided whether they could be used for slave labor or were to be sent to the "showers"—that is, gas chambers. A few were chosen for work, but the great majority were sent directly to take a "shower".

Since I and the rest of the girls from the last boxcar had apparently been pre-selected, we were separated from the rest and sent directly to a barrack. I was still clutching my little suitcase, and was still in a state of shock. I have only fuzzy recollections of those traumatic days.

The one thing that I can never forget is the smoke belching out of the nearby tall chimneys, permeating the whole camp with a sickening stench. At first we couldn't identify this awful odor, but we were soon told by those who had been there for a few days that we might as well get used to the smell of burning human bodies. Fortunately, I wasn't there long enough to get used to it. A few days after my arrival at Auschwitz, I was sent to a slave labor camp, which was to be my world until the end of the war.

Larch Ludwigsdorf concentration camp (one of 97 sub-camps of Gross-Rosen) was situated in low, wooded mountains near the Czech border. Before the war this scenic area was popular among city dwellers, who came here to relax, and to soak in the many spas in the region. Unfortunately, I and my fellow prisoners, who had no idea where we were, had not been brought here to enjoy the natural beauty, nor to soak in the spas, and we were much too traumatized to notice any beauty in the surroundings. Pulling into the camp, the sight that greeted us did nothing to calm our fears. We were ordered to line up in the dirt yard, and counted, as always, just in case one of us might have vanished during the heavily guarded trip. We were flanked on either side by rows of crude barracks, made of unfinished boards. A double electrified fence surrounded the compound, with armed guard towers at the corners. A fence down the middle separated the men's camp from the women's camp.

As in any Nazi camp, it was obvious that there were two classes of people inhabiting the camp: the masters and the slaves. I was about to join the slaves, and the masters never hesitated to remind me of which group I belonged to. All of us slaves had one thing in common: we were all Jews. Just as putting us in cattle cars didn't mean that the Nazis thought of us as cattle, using us for slave labor didn't mean they thought of us as slaves. No slave owner would be so stupid as to starve, murder, and needlessly torture his valuable workers. To the Nazis we were vermin, deserving of no more than the cruelest treatment. On the other hand, our Nazi masters appeared to be fine specimens of humanity–all dressed in their immaculate gray-green uniforms, with shining boots and buttons. They carried themselves very erect, looked well fed and in perfect health. In contrast to these elite members of the self-appointed Master Race, the inmates were a pathetic lot, who had been judged to be sub-human, and to an outsider they would have appeared to be sub-human. Those who moved at all, shuffled along in ragged, filthy, gray garments. Many though, just sat on the ground, staring blankly at nothing in particular. Some were so emaciated that I wondered how they could still be alive. To top it off, a large number of this lower class were colored from head to toe in green, red or black, which on this my first day I couldn't understand. I would find out soon enough. The lower class was actually divided into two levels; a few of the prisoners appeared better dressed and better fed, and also carried some form of club. These were the kapos, who were rewarded with a better life by seeing to it that the rest were kept in line, by whatever means it took. Kapos had to demonstrate a willingness to resort to brutality in order to keep their positions. Any kapo who displayed any sign of mercy could easily be replaced. For the Nazis, having absolute control over life and death of all these wretched beings, kapos and regular prisoners alike, served them well in reinforcing their feeling of superiority.

As I later discovered, just out of sight, over a ridge, was the camp burial ground, which acquired new bodies on a daily basis. Each morning a detail came around and carried off the bodies of those who hadn't survived the night. An inmate might end up in this plot by being shot, hanged, beaten to death, or dying of dysentery or just hunger and exhaustion. Another cause of death was from being poisoned by the colored powders that I had been brought here to work with, be covered with, and constantly inhale. I can say that I was actually lucky to be put to work with the green powder– the life-expectancy for those who worked with the red powder was a few months at the most. But all this knowledge was still to come, and I was simply scared and bewildered on my first day, as I stood there helpless with the rest of the new young women.

With the usual, "Macht schnell", "Verfluchte Juden" and other assorted curses, we were marched to our new "home" in one of the barracks. At our barrack we were each issued a gray uniform dress with a yellow Star of David on the front and on the back. There was no attempt to match the size of the dress to the size of the receiver. As a result, there was a lot of trading among the girls. Still, when all the swapping was done, my uniform was still much too big, and I was forced to resort to a makeshift drawstring to keep it from falling off of my small body.

All the barracks were filled with two-tiered bunks, with two girls sleeping together on each bunk. The bunks had mattress of straw stuffed into a bag of ticking, and one blanket each. It was now late in the afternoon, so we weren't sent to work that first day. When the girls who had finished the day shift returned, we were all called out for roll call, and then lined up for the evening "meal". I had to subsist on this same "meal", which was nothing more than a bowl of watery soup, every day for the rest of my stay in the camp. By now I was maybe a semi-zombie, as my feelings were starting to surface, and I missed my family so badly that it hurt to the bone.

The next morning we were ordered outside to be lined up, and counted, and introduced to the "breakfast" that I was to expect for the duration of my stay at the camp. This consisted of a slice of bread and a cup of ersatz coffee. Anyone caught saving a little of this bread for later in the day was subject to severe punishment. But a lot of us took this risk, because we got so hungry before our 12 hour shift was over.

Having finished our breakfast, we were marched to work. We walked for about an hour up a steep hill along a zigzag and switch-backed trail through a forest until we passed some outlying buildings before we reached the factory area. Our SS masters and the kapos kept the column moving swiftly by delivering a solid kick or a blow with their rubber truncheons to anyone who slowed down. If our guards heard someone talking, the guilty party would also get whacked.

The factory wasn't one large building, but rather a network of very small units spread out over a large area on a hillside. Each unit was either dug into the side of the hill or partially dug in and its roof covered with sod, so the whole complex just looked like part of the forest from the air. This hill was the site of an abandoned coal mine, and was riddled with tunnels, which the Germans utilized to connect different parts of the complex. The coal mine had been abandoned in 1937 because of excessive methane gas.

Probably the most pathetic sight I have ever witnessed was the treatment of the men who were forced to push large carts of steaming food all the way from the camp to the factory, so that the Germans could have a hot lunch. For this grueling labor the Nazis selected those men who appeared to be almost skeletons, who were suffering from dysentery, and occasionally had to pause to vomit. The Aryan Supermen walked along beside them, beating them with clubs when they showed any sign of slowing down. This scene was a sickening reminder of the kind of monsters who were in control of our lives. The officers who oversaw this barbarity all day, had no problem going home at night to sip fine wine, listen to classical music, and lavish affection upon their dogs and cats, and then get up the next morning to inflect the same torture on the wretched prisoners. Who were the sub-humans?

At the factory, we girls worked in small teams assembling various forms of explosives and ammunition, under the strict supervision of our kapos from the barracks. I was assigned to a group of six girls working in a small room containing drums of green powder and a balance scale. Our job was to weigh out a specified amount of the powder, put it in a small press to compact it, take the now formed powder out of the press and measure its height to be sure it met the required specifications, and finally pass it on to be assembled into products such as land mines.

Long before the end of the first day, we were all covered with green powder, which we quickly discovered would not wash out of our hair, clothes, bodies, or anything else. The powder was very bitter, and when we spat the spittle was green. As we returned to the barracks after the first day at work, one SS man greeted us with a laugh: "You were a bunch of pretty girls when you left, but look at you now." Other girls were apparently working with different explosives, since some came back looking red or black, as well as green. Worst of all, the powder–no matter what color—burned our eyes and irritated our lungs. Of course, this was of no concern to our German overseers in the factories, since they all wore protective masks and clothing.

The work wasn't only bad for our health, but it was also dangerous, and we were driven mercilessly by our overseers. Luckily for me, after several weeks of work with the powder, suddenly one day a German woman came up to me and told me to follow her, which of course I did. She took me over to another building, which turned out to be an electronic assembly facility, where she was a supervisor. This plant was exceedingly cleaner than the land mine factory, and employed mainly older women from Germany (not Jews). She put me to work, and said that I would now be working for her. This was great, as far as I was concerned. The work was no easier, but I was out of that awful powder. Surprisingly, I was the only Jewish worker in this unit. Besides the German women, there were Polish, Slavic, Russian, and Ukrainian girls working there. These girls were paid workers, not prisoners. Most of them lived in the camp, but they were free to go into town when their shifts were finished. Most of the Polish girls went home on the weekends.

It wasn't long before my supervisor at the green powder unit discovered that I was missing. As soon as she found out where I was, she stormed over there and told me that I was working for her, and had to go back with her right then. Much as I preferred my new, much cleaner job, I had no choice but to go with her. However, I had hardly gotten back before the supervisor from the electronics factory came rushing into the powder factory looking for me. Now, the most incredible thing happened. As I watched in astonishment, these two German women got into a violent argument, which actually turned into a shoving match, over who would have me, a lowly Jew, working for her. I would never have believed such a scenario if I hadn't seen it with my own eyes. Somehow, the woman from the electronics unit won the argument, and I happily followed my new German mistress back to the cleaner job. However this wasn't a permanent victory, from then on I was shuttled back and forth between the two jobs.

No matter where I worked, the rest of my daily life was still the same, including the rigorous, exhausting march to and from the factory. Of all the physical torments of my life in the camp, the worst was the constant, agonizing hunger. For the entire time of my nearly three years in Ludwigsdorf, I subsisted on a piece of bread and a cup of ersatz coffee in the morning, and a cup of watery soup in the evening. Sometimes the soup had a bit of squash or potato in it; but usually it was devoid of any solids. I would say that most of the time it was just boiled grass. One time, one of the Polish girls I worked with felt sorry for me, and smuggled a small beet into the factory to give to me. The fact that it was covered with dirt and sand was of no importance; this was red gold. I quickly slipped over to the toilet, and devoured this precious gift, to avoid any possibility that it might be discovered and confiscated from me, and that I would be beaten for possessing this contraband.

Sometimes I would sneak over to the garbage cans at night, and scavenge for any bit of something edible. The finding of so little as a dirty potato peel made the treasure hunt a success. I had to, "sneak over," because stealing garbage was a crime for which I would have been beaten if caught, but my hunger was so unbearable that I was willing to take the chance.

And then there was the ever-present mental torment of simply being a prisoner and a slave, and having all freedom denied. Sometimes I would look out through the barred window in the back of our barrack, and watch birds flitting from branch to branch, and I thought, "Oh, how lucky they are." I wondered if they appreciated the fact that no one was ordering them when and where to fly, on pain of death if they disobeyed. Occasionally I would see a deer, peacefully browsing just beyond the fence outside my window. How I envied that deer, and would ask myself, "Why couldn't I just be a deer, and run free in the forest, free of this nightmare?"

By far the worst anguish I suffered, and suffered constantly, was my separation from my family. At home, I always knew I loved my mother very deeply, but I didn't realize how much all my family meant to me until they were taken away. We had arguments and jealousies like everyone else, but when the chips were down we were the *Family*. I'm sure that being part of a hated and persecuted minority greatly strengthened the bond between us, and this made separation doubly painful. It didn't take long for almost every girl in the camp to develop a very close friendship with one of the other girls. This was a key to survival. It was very common for loners in the camps, whether men or women, to lose the will to live, and just waste away.

My special friend was Perka, a very pretty, intelligent girl from Sosnowiec, who was just a little older than I was. We were like sisters, only closer, because of the strong need we had for each other's support. We shared everything: our straw mattress and blanket, and any extra food we could find, but far more importantly, we helped close that aching wound in both our hearts from being separated from our families. I have to confess that even after being so intimate for almost three years, I don't remember her last name; inside the barracks we always went by first names and to the Germans we were just numbers.

I was also lucky to have another friend in camp, Zosza Kaufman, who was from Bendzin and was a friend of Yossel. Being a little older, she looked after me as much as she could. She was somewhat like a big sister and played an important part in my survival.

To make our lives even more miserable, the prisoners were assembled and painstakingly counted three times a day: morning, at the end of work, and upon return to the camp. These countings were agonizing; we had to stand in the rain and bitter cold, and of course we never had any protection from the weather but our thin prisoner smocks. Sometimes we were forced to stand for an hour or more, while some of the girls who were too weak from starvation and sickness would pass out. Usually these poor souls would be dragged off to the sick room, which was little more than a way station for the burial ground.

Also at the counts, any extra food or other prohibited valuables were confiscated, and the "dirty Jew" was beaten as a lesson to the rest of the less than human inmates. If the count were even one person off, it would start all over again until the discrepancy was resolved. The Germans valued our work, but they didn't value our lives, because they knew there was a huge supply of potential replacements being slaughtered every day in Death Camps all over Poland.

In the nearly three years I spent in Ludwigsdorf camp, I never had any hot water, never had any soap, never had any clothes except the gray prison-issued uniforms, never had a day off work, never had any meals except for the bread, watery soup and ersatz coffee, and never had a coat–and it got bitterly cold in winter. Those of us who were up to it, found some relief from the misery by singing together. When we felt most depressed at night, we would sing about the end of the war, of our own release from the suffering of the camp, and of our dreams for the future.

We had a little hope for the future, but as the sound of our feeble, pathetic voices floated over the camp walls, over the guards and dogs, over the electric fence, anyone listening in at the time might have wondered how we could find the inner strength to sing at all. Those of us who resolved to make the best of this inescapable Hell were by and large the ones who survived; while those who lived in constant despair were much less likely to hold on to the end.

Marching to and from work, we were required to walk four abreast; which had an unintended benefit for us, in that if one of us were especially weak that day, she could be placed in the middle of the row and held up by the others, who for that day were stronger. Every girl, including me, had her days in the middle of the row and her days on the outside. The result was that many of the girls survived who otherwise might not have.

When I arrived in camp, I had a fine new pair of shoes, but the long rough walk, to and from work, in all kinds of weather, soon wore them completely to shreds. We might never have gotten replacements, except for the fact that the gas chambers were providing thousands of excess shoes every day. Periodically a truck would pull up in the compound, and a huge box of loose shoes, which I believe were taken usually from Jews murdered in Auschwitz, would be dumped in the barracks, and there would be a mad scramble as we all searched for a pair that fit. Of course, if one shoe was found to fit, its mate could be anywhere in the pile, and often was never found, so we felt lucky to have two shoes that were close to fitting.

Later on, we were given wooden clogs, which were not at all suitable for walking, especially in the snow. Plodding up the long trail to work, weakened as I was by starvation, every step demanded all the strength I could muster, but as the snow collected thicker and thicker on the bottom of my clogs it soon made walking so difficult that I could barely move, to say nothing of keeping up with the column. Falling behind brought on a rain of blows from the guards, so I had no choice but to take off these hated clogs, and trudge barefoot through the snow. I have never understood why I didn't lose my feet, or at least my toes, to frostbite. Perhaps I should thank the guards for marching us at maximum speed.

One day after working in the electronics factory for only a few weeks, a German woman came up to me during a break, then after glancing around to be sure no one else was watching, she began to cry softly. She said that she felt very bad about what I was going through, especially because I reminded her of her own daughter, back home, who was about my age. As she walked away, she pressed a piece of bread into my hand.

On my pathetic rations, I had become very pale and thin, and I dreamed of food constantly. This piece of bread was like a gift from Heaven, but it also put me in some danger. I knew that if I were caught with it I would no doubt be beaten. I immediately went to the toilet room and gobbled the bread down as fast as I could, a task made more difficult because my mouth was dry from fear. I had to make sure that there were no telltale crumbs and no sign of chewing when I emerged from the toilet. As soon as I finished, I was out of there and headed back to work. However, I wasn't fast enough; the guard outside the toilet had an eagle eye open for any slackers, and I was judged to have taken too long. The result was several painful blows from the guard's club, but on balance it was worth it to have that extra bit of bread. Even more valuable was the act of kindness I received from this German woman. That was something really special.

On another occasion, I was cleaning up in the back when I felt so tired that I lay down and fell asleep, and didn't wake up until the end of my shift. When I went to my kapo and confessed that I had fallen asleep, she said that they had been looking all over for me and I was very, very lucky, because she was just about to report me as missing. I barely missed a good thrashing that day.

One event that I will certainly never forget came about while we were measuring powder for landmines. The scale we used to weigh the powder broke. We could tell that it wasn't working properly, because no matter how much powder we put on it, it showed the same weight. We knew this could be dangerous, so we told the foreman that the scale was broken and asked him to fix it before we used it any more. The foreman told us to quit complaining and get back to work before he taught us a lesson with his club.

On this same day we happened to be greatly honored by the presence of a high-ranking officer from the Master Race—tall, lean, and erect in his immaculate field gray uniform–surrounded by sycophants. For one of us low creatures to get caught just looking at this demigod would have bought us a beating. He was in the camp to make sure that the lowly Poles and sub-human Jews were doing a proper job for their masters. As bad luck would have it, during his inspection the press blew up, because the powder was incorrectly measured as a result of the faulty scale. This brought immediate and tragic consequences for us workers. The foreman immediately accused all six of us girls, who were working near the press, of the dreaded charge: "sabotage." We knew that this was an offense punishable by certain death. Although I knew that I and the other girls were completely innocent, I also knew that this didn't matter to the Nazis. In our experience, the Germans never hesitated to hang someone, guilty or not, as an example to the other prisoners. In fact, they obviously enjoyed the spectacle.

With this accusation, I was thrown into a state of panic, as I'm sure the other five girls were. I was sure that this was my last day on Earth, and I thought of my family, and how I would never see them again. Since the beginning of the war, I had seen little reason to believe that God was listening to the prayers of any Jew, so why should He listen to me now? But for all the long, winding descent back to the barracks, I prayed every step of the way, more fervently than ever before in my life. "Please God, don't let my life end now, in this awful way. Please spare me until this nightmare is over, and I can see my mother and the rest of my family again. O God, what can I say to you so that you will spare me? I want to live, but I know this is the end. Nothing can save me."

When we got back to the barracks there was an announcement of a special assembly. Everyone in the camp was ordered out into the yard to observe—and supposedly to profit from—the punishment of the "saboteurs". My kapo came over to me and said, "You were born on Christmas Day; maybe that will bring you luck."

I was too much in shock to appreciate her attempt to salve my fears– I didn't feel the least bit hopeful. I was shaking like a birch leaf. Then, our punishment was announced: we were each to be severely beaten with a rubber club. I couldn't believe my ears— could it really be true–was it my prayers? I think God was on vacation at that time. Did the Nazis' consciences bother them because they knew we were innocent? What consciences? Did the accident of my birth date have any effect? I think not. I believe the real answer is simpler–the Germans needed our labor. Besides, a severe beating was almost as good for an example to the other prisoners as a hanging, which they had seen plenty of. Normally, being savagely beaten would not be something to be pleased about, but the six of us were more than extremely relieved–our lives, which we had conceded were over, had just been spared. We felt that we could survive the beating, however severe. We would live at least another day.

I was ordered to strip off my rag uniform, and to bend over a small table to receive my beating, which was reluctantly administered by my Kapo. After the first 10 blows, the German in charge called a halt, and berated the Kapo for not beating me hard enough. He told her that if she didn't know how to give a proper flogging, he would teach her by demonstrating on her. He ordered her to start over, and this time to do it with some vigor. Every blow from this rubber club tore more and more flesh from my back while I screamed at every excruciating stroke. Following the beating I was shoved to the ground, a bloody mess, completely unable to move. Somebody picked me up and dumped me into an empty room by myself. The other five girls received the same brutal treatment.

It would have been unthinkable for the Germans to allow anyone clean my wounds or to give me any food or water. I wouldn't have been able to eat, anyway. Because of the intense pain, I couldn't even think about sleeping. After a long, almost unbearable night, the next morning the kapo came in and informed me that I had to go to work as usual that day, or go to the sickroom. I knew better than to ask to go to the sickroom. Going there was nearly always a one-way trip. The Germans had no use for anyone who couldn't work, so they frequently evacuated the sickroom by tossing the bodies of those who had died during the night into a truck and sending them to the burial ground behind the hill, and those still alive, who usually resembled skeletons more than people, were shipped to Auschwitz to be gassed. If I wanted to live, I had to go to work, no matter how painful; so I forced myself to get up, and made the long march up the hill to the factory. My five pain racked girlfriends all made the same choice. We could never have made this march on our own power, but were saved by the healthier girls getting on either side of each of us and practically carrying us up. As I struggled through the day to do my work, every little movement ignited more sharp pain. I kept trying to tell myself, "The worst is almost over, and I'm very lucky that I'm still alive."

One day in the midst of my misery and despair, something wonderful happened: I got remarkably good news about my family. This came about through the cunning and bravery of my brother Yossel who, unknown to me, was now a Pole named Jusek. Until this time I had no way of knowing if any of my family were alive or dead. As the months passed during which the rest of the family was waiting in their Ghetto hiding place, with no final word from Mietek about Magdeburg, Jusek and Mother had begun traveling around on trains. Jusek chose some of these train trips to pass through Ludwigsdorf, in attempt to make contact with me. The family knew of my internment in Ludwigsdorf, because when we first arrived in the camp, we were allowed, and even required, to write home to tell our families how nicely we were being treated.

Walking around in Ludwigsdorf, as my brother did, was not like a stroll in the park. Not only was there the lager, where I was imprisoned, near to the town, but there was also a large German Army hospital. Trainloads of wounded soldiers from the Russian front were pouring into the station every day, and the whole area was swarming with German military. Jusek recognized that he was in constant jeopardy, and must, at all cost, avoid drawing any attention to himself. As he had experienced in the past, the best way to avoid suspicion was to display an air as though he were completely comfortable in his surrounding, and had every right to be there. To pull this off was no small feat, for he was terrified the whole time, but he succeeded, as he was never questioned by anyone.

Mietek and Jusek had created forged Polish papers not just for themselves, but also for the rest of the family, including me, and Yossel wanted to let me know that if I could escape, he had these papers ready. Jusek's method of contacting me was, as usual, inventive and daring. On the train he made the acquaintance of a girl named Katerina, who worked in the same camp where I was a slave, but being Polish, she was allowed to live outside the camp. He flirted with her, and cultivated her affection. By the time of his next visit, she had fallen in love with this handsome young "Polish" man, and she was very willing to help him. Yossel "casually" asked Katerina if she might happen to know of a girl in the camp by the name of Dora Szpringer, who was a "friend of a friend of his". She answered that she not only knew me, but also worked in my area. What a stroke of luck! Jusek was now certain that he had a means to smuggle a note to me. He told Katerina that he would be really grateful if she could do his "friend" a favor, by delivering a letter to me. She agreed to be the messenger, which while being relatively easy, was quite dangerous. If she were caught, we would both be in serious trouble, especially me.

The next morning in the factory, an excited Katerina whispered to me that she had something for me, and to meet her in the toilet. I followed her there, where she slipped me the letter from my brother Yossel (now going by the name Jusek). This amazing letter told me that all of the family members (except my brother Issa, whose whereabouts were unknown) were still alive and that he had Polish papers prepared for me, and that he had a plan to hide me if I could escape. He would be waiting for my answer, which could be sent through Katerina. Nothing could have warmed my heart and raised my spirits than the incredible news that my family was still alive. Oh, how I ached to fly over the deadly barbed wire and hug my dear brother Yossel. But I was faced with a life and death decision. On the one hand, life in the camp was almost unbearable, and I knew that any time, particularly if I were injured or became sick, a truck could pull into the compound and haul me off to the gas chamber. On the other hand, I just could not envision any plan that would get me past the fence, the guards, and the dogs. A failed attempt meant certain death. After much painful deliberation, I had to face the reality that for now I really had no choice. I couldn't see any way I could escape without being caught. Miserable as my life was, I was alive and I wanted to stay that way as long as possible, so I made the choice to bide my time until an escape plan came along with a reasonable chance of succeeding. I tearfully disposed of the letter in the toilet and sent word back to Jusek, via Katerina, that I couldn't try to escape at this time. I would have to take my chances inside and leave my fate in the hands of God.

Jusek got word back to me that he understood, but that he couldn't linger in the area any longer; therefore he left, and I was again alone in the camp–but with uplifted spirits and renewed hope. I never did get to see Jusek while he was in Ludwigsdorf, but he did see me once. He went out on the tall railroad trestle that passed by the route up to the factories, and was able to pick me out in the group trudging up the hill. When he told Mother, she insisted that he take her to where she could see me; an idea that Jusek thought was way too risky, but Mother was Mother and she would have her way; so he brought her to a place where she could see us walking, but she was too far away to make out which one I was. It saddens me to think of the anguish my dear mother must have suffered, seeing those wretched slaves, all covered with green powder, and knowing that her little Dora was one of them.

My choice not to try to escape undoubtedly saved my life. The camp was surrounded by guards, by dogs, and by an electric fence. Beyond those barriers, virtually insurmountable in themselves, lay an unfriendly countryside, where anyone who even tried to help me would be setting himself up for certain death if caught. Of course, at the time the choice seemed incredibly difficult to me and there were many days and nights during which I wondered if I had made the right choice. Even though I couldn't be with my family, just knowing that they were alive did wonders for my morale. My boosted morale helped me to endure the endless, tormenting days of camp life.

As the days of spring 1945 dragged on, the sound of planes overhead and bombs falling all around became more and more frequent, and we heard more rumors that the Russian Army was getting close. The arrogance of the guards slowly turned to fear. Unlike the early years of the war, now everyone knew that Germany was going to lose the war. One day the guards announced that the next day there was going to be an evacuation of the camp, starting at midnight, and we were to be marched to an undisclosed destination. We had all heard enough rumors to know what this meant. This meant marching all day, with little or no food, and no stopping except when the guards needed a rest; just marching, day after day until most of the marchers would be dead from exhaustion or shot for falling behind. There would be no excuse for not keeping up or stopping for any reason, you would simply be killed. This was going to be a "death march". The "death march" was a method commonly used by the Germans, near the end of the war, to evacuate a concentration camp.

Having no choice, we girls prepared to start out. No one slept; we were all much too scared to even think of sleeping. Midnight came and went with no sign of any guards. A few trucks were heard and seen beyond the electric fence, but overall there was an eerie stillness around the camp. No dogs barked, no sounds were heard, no guards even checked the door.

Dawn rose the next morning, and we still heard nothing, but we were afraid to open the door to see what was happening. Then suddenly the door opened and instead of the usual German guards, Russian soldiers came through the door, announcing in Russian, "You are free."

Polish and Russian are close enough that we Polish girls understood what they had said. Our lives had been spared, there would be no death march, but there was no sudden rejoicing, for it was such a shock we were afraid to believe it. Was this some kind of Nazi dirty trick? It didn't seem possible that such a major event could happen so suddenly and simply–yet it had. We had to go outside to see for ourselves that the Germans had actually gone. Sure enough, there were no Germans to be seen, only Russians.

Finally accepting my freedom as real, I went out through the open gate, and started to run. I ran until my weakened body could run no more and flopped down on the grass. Then I asked myself, "Where am I running to? There is nowhere for me to go. I can't just run back to Bendzin."

So my run to freedom had lasted only until I had run out of breath, and having no other realistic option, I walked slowly back to the camp. In some camps that the Russians liberated, the soldiers had acted like wild animals and raped the women inmates, but we were lucky. The Russians treated us humanely, but didn't give us food. They were too busy chasing the fleeing Germans to worry about us. We were on our own to get what food we could scrounge from what the Germans had left. Within a couple of days the Red Cross showed up and gave us real food–and lots of it–and hot. But our stomachs were not used to so much rich food, and all of the girls got very sick. Under the care of the Red Cross we were treated for our various illnesses and began to get our strength back. Little by little the girls began to leave for their homes—if they still existed.

CHAPTER TWENTY FOUR

A New Life Begins

I was in such shock at the time, that I have no memory of how or when I returned to Bendzin. All I know is that I got there, and I assume it must have been by train. I can't even remember if I was excited to go back or not. If I was, the excitement was certainly dampened when I got there.

The Bendzin I had known and loved was totally changed. Not so much physically, for most of the buildings were still there, but inside the buildings and on the streets I saw only Polish faces. There were a very small number of Jews to be seen, but none that I recognized. The major difference was the absence of Jewish life— the smell of gefilte fish and other distinctly Jewish foods was absent, and the sounds of talking and arguing in Yiddish were nowhere to be heard in the old Jewish neighborhood. The synagogue was completely gone, along with the Jewish market, and of special importance for me, the house where I was born, and our family store. There was nothing about this city to make me feel at home, or even welcome.

Going to my family's former home, I found, as I had expected, that a Polish family had moved in. The steps that my family and I had so emotionally kissed the night after the selection in the sports stadium were still there, the same steps, yet my feeling about them was totally different. I stood outside my own house, which now was not my own house anymore, not knowing what to do or where to go. Instead of joy, my homecoming brought only tears of despair. The joy I had felt at liberation was now buried beneath a dense blanket of fear and confusion. I didn't even know if I had any family left alive. The Jewish culture that had given me such a feeling of belonging was dead. For me, my beloved hometown of Bendzin, although full of Polish people, was the "City of Ghosts."

Of the hundred or so people who lived in our apartment building, I know of only four persons, besides our family, who were alive at the end of the war. One of these, a young woman from a family who made hats in their home, survived Auschwitz and came home only to find that she was the only one alive from her entire family. She hanged herself.

I found out later what had happened to our shoe store. In January, 1945, with the Germans obviously losing and Russians getting ever closer, Josef Jarosz felt it wise to flee the city, so he caught the last train headed west out of Bendzin, but before he disappeared he burned our shoe store to the ground. We later learned that even a year after the last of us had left, rumors were still afloat that we were somehow alive, and Jarosz just couldn't bear the thought of our returning and getting our store back. So he apparently burned it down out of spite.

While wandering the streets of Bendzin, in my state of bewilderment, I saw a Jewish girl of my age coming my way. She rushed up to me cried "Oh Dora, I'm so thrilled to see you're alive!"

It was obvious that she knew me, but I had no idea who she was. My awkward silence soon made it apparent to her, that I didn't recognize her. The bright look on her face changed to one of puzzlement and disappointment.

"Dora, don't you know me? I'm your girlfriend—Lola. I sat next to you in school."

Try as I might, I could not remember knowing Lola. Her face seemed vaguely familiar, but her name meant nothing to me, and I simply could not place her. To escape from what was quickly becoming an embarrassment for both of us, I blurted out," Of course I remember you, Lola. You just surprised me. It's been such a long time since I've seen anyone I know."

I'm not sure that I convinced her, but I certainly hope so. As for myself, as hard as I've tried in the ensuing years, to this day, I've never been able to recall who she was, and it still bothers me.

A few Jews who had been liberated earlier by the Russians, and had made it back to Bendzin, formed a Reunion Committee, and began collecting names of survivors as they returned, as well as any other information that would help people find their loved ones. They also had the unpleasant task of passing along, to the returnees, any information that they received about those family members who would never return, which was, of course, the vast majority of the Jews of Bendzin.

At this point, I had no idea what to do with myself. I had no way of knowing my family's whereabouts, or if they were even alive. The changes that I saw in Bendzin didn't come as a surprise to my conscious mind, but emotionally I wasn't prepared. After spending the last three years dreaming of home and family, the shock of the reality was too much for me, and I was thrown into a state of hopelessness and depression. Having no home and no one I knew to talk with, the more I stayed in Bendzin, the more depressed I became. I just wanted to get away. But where to? I decided to go back to the camp at Ludwigsdorf, where former prisoners were still being fed and housed. When and if any of my family came to Bendzin, the Committee would tell them where I was, and they could either come to me, or send for me. All of them knew where Ludwigsdorf was, except for Issa, and if came back from Russia he could easily find out. I dreaded to go back to my place of suffering, but I saw no better option, so I hopped on the next train headed that way, and returned to the only place where, in my present state of aloneness, I could feel any sense of security. How ironic—my seeking refuge in the place that had been a living Hell for me, and from which I had prayed for deliverance for the past three years.

When Father and Moishe arrived in Bendzin, a few days after I had left, they checked with the Committee, and learned that I had gone back to the camp at Ludwigsdorf. Since there was no news yet of the other family members, they also left for Ludwigsdorf to reunite with me. Finding me was no problem, and we enjoyed a warm and tearful reunion. The next and urgent business at hand was to find some decent place to live. Since Ludwigsdorf was a very small town, Father thought that our prospects would be better in Nowa Ruda, a neighboring small city.

Father and Moishe went to the Polish Mayor of Nowa Ruda, hoping he would help them. Aware that being known to be a Jew might be a detriment among Poles, Moishe used his identity as Mietek Scrowronski. The mayor was very helpful, offering them space in the front house of a two-house villa. The owner, and current occupant, was a Nazi who owned a large textile factory across the road from the houses. This Nazi was in no position to question anything he was told to do. The three of us moved into the downstairs portion of the front house, and the owner's family moved upstairs. His mother was living in the other house.

We settled in, and prayed for the arrival of the rest of the family. Since Yossel had visited Father, we had good reason to be optimistic about his safety, as well as Mother, and Laya, but we had no clue as to what had happened to Issa. Very shortly thereafter, a Russian officer and some of his troops came to the house, kicked the Nazi out, and moved into the upstairs. I found myself sharing the kitchen with Russian soldiers. Having heard many stories of the widespread rape of young women by Russian troops, I was more than a little uneasy in this situation; however, they were always very courteous to me. Maybe I reminded them of a little sister back home.

CHAPTER TWENTY FIVE

Reunion

Our prayers for a family reunion were soon to be partially answered. With the war ended, Issa desperately sought to return home; however, the Soviets seemed to be in no hurry to grant him permission to leave Russia. At long last, he got permission, and climbed aboard a train, arriving in Bendzin just a few days after Father and Moishe had left for Nova Ruda. But it wasn't the same town he remembered. It was a whole new world he was entering, and the old world was wiped away as though it had never existed. He saw no Jews on the streets, only Poles. Finally, he did run into a Jewish friend of his from before the war. They recognized each other and embraced. The first words the friend spoke were, "Issa, you are a lucky guy!"

Issa look at him and said, "What're you joking about? I came to look for my family and you're joking about it?"

His friend repeated, "You're a lucky guy!"

"Don't Joke"

The friend hadn't realized that since Issa had been away in Russia since 1939, he might not know what had gone on in Poland and the rest of Europe; maybe Issa hadn't even heard that the murderous swine had wiped out most of the Jews of Europe, including almost all of the Jews of Bendzin, that most families had been annihilated, that the few individuals who survived were lucky if they found a brother or sister still alive. Still laughing with excitement, his friend replied in earnest:

"No, you have your father, you have your mother, you have your sisters, you have your brothers. You are the only one family from the whole European Jewish People."

Issa got angry. "What are you laughing about?"

"Don't get angry. It's a true thing. If you don't believe me, I will go with you tomorrow where your father is the mayor of the city." Of course he wasn't the mayor; this must have been some rumor.

"Good, I'll go with you."

So they went the next day to Nova Ruda, and were walking around when suddenly they saw a man walking. His friend says, "Do you know that guy?"

"No"

"That's your brother."

"My brother? That's my brother?"

"Yes. Don't say nothin'. I want to see if he'll recognize you."

They walked toward Moishe, and the friend and Moishe exchanged greetings from a short distance. All the time Moishe was eyeing Issa. Then the friend whispered to Issa, "I think he recognizes you."

Cautiously Moishe approached them and asked, "Are you Issa?"

"Yes"

Moishe grabbed Issa in a bear hug.

We can't be too surprised at their mutual lack of instant recognition. The hard lives they had endured since parting, more than five years ago, had aged them both considerably. Plus, Issa had never seen Moishe so tanned and without glasses, and Moishe had never seen his older brother so thin.

"Issa, come with me. I'll show you where we live, me and our father and Dora. I want to see if she recognizes you."

As they entered the kitchen, where I was working, Moishe excitedly announced, "Dora, I just met this man on the street. "Do you know who this is?"

"No."

"This is Issa's best friend."

I grabbed him and held on to him. "Where is Issa? When is he coming? Are you hungry? Come in and sit down. Tell me all about Issa. When did you see him? How do you know him?"

"I worked with him in Siberia."

The "stranger" was answering my questions with a perfect poker face. I took little notice of Moishe, who was sitting next to me, grinning like the Cheshire cat and straining to keep from bursting out laughing. I repeated my questions.
"Did you see him recently?"

"Yes, I saw him very recently."

"Do you know where he is?"

Issa, feeling that the prank had been played out, stood up and said, in a mildly exasperated tone,

"Dora, you silly goose, *I am* Issa!"

I sat there for a few seconds, wondering if this could be true. If this were really my brother, how could I have not recognized him? I was so confused I didn't know what to believe. I wanted to believe him, but I had to be sure, so I asked him something only my family would know:

"If you are my brother, tell me something about me when I was a child."

Issa very patiently replied, "When you were about four years old, you were very sick and couldn't walk, so Mother took you to Busko Zdroj for a cure."

With all doubt removed, I jumped up and threw my arms around him. Why hadn't I recognized him? I still wonder about that. It was also good for my spirits to see that the Germans and the Russians, with all of their cruelty, hadn't destroyed Issa's great sense of humor.

A few minutes later, when Father came in, Moishe tried to play the same trick on him, saying, "Father, this man knows Issa."

Father just looked at him as though he were daft, and said, "What are you talking about? This is Issa."

Moishe should have known better than to think my father would not know his own son.

While the four of us were celebrating our reunion, the remaining three family members were finding it more difficult to get back to Poland. Much as they wanted to get out of Germany, the simple fact was that no transportation existed out of the American Zone going to the East. There wasn't much they could do, except wait for such transportation to become available. Yossel spent his days moving about the city in an effort to get a grasp of the overall situation, and learn what he could about anything that would help the family to make a life in the new world in which we all found ourselves. He would occasionally meet another Jew, which was always an emotionally rewarding experience. Whenever a Jew would meet a person, whom he thought was probably another Jew, he wouldn't feel comfortable to come right out and ask, "Are you Jewish?"

The other party might not take this query kindly if he were a Gentile. Therefore, the common practice came to be, simply saying, in an interrogative tone, "Amchu?"

This Hebrew word meaning, "the people," would be understood by any Jew, but would mean nothing to a Gentile.

Finally, the long awaited day came. Mother, Yossel and Laya packed up as many valuables as they could carry, and climbed aboard an extremely crowed train bound for Poland. The train was, of course, packed to overflowing. As many people as possible were crammed into the coaches, with the remainder hanging on to the sides, or riding on the roof. Being on the outside was quite risky, especially for those on the roof when the train passed through a tunnel. This was particularly dangerous at night, when they had very short notice before having to hug the roof of the train, until it cleared the tunnel. Both Yossel and Laya spent their fair share of time on the outside, which Yossel thought was great sport, but Laya was just plain scared. She had been deprived of all fun in her life for the past six years, but this was not her idea of how to make up for that loss.

Anticipating that finding food during the trip would be a problem, Mother brought as many edibles as she could schlep, including a large open bucket of strawberry jam. As was almost inevitable, in the ultra-crowded carriage, one of their fellow travelers accidentally stuck his foot in the bucket of jam. This precipitated a free-for-all, whereby, everybody who could get close enough was busily engaged in scraping the jam from the culprit's upraised foot, and licking it off their fingers. Many of these folks hadn't tasted such a delicacy in years, and were not about to see it go to waste.

Upon reaching Bendzin, they checked in with the Committee, and wasted little time in heading on to Ludwigsdorf. After nearly six horrible, perilous years, my family was all together once more. It is impossible to describe our joy at this reunion.

Our euphoria, however, was soon tempered by reality. We could not just simply hang around in our villa in Nowa Ruda forever. We must all make new lives for ourselves, and it could not be in Bendzin, where the Poles had taken over all the homes and business formerly owned by Jews, and our whole culture had been wiped out. We felt no desire to return there, plus we had no doubt but that any attempt by us to recover our property would have been met with serious resistance and likely violence. In fact, all of Poland was still rife with anti-Semitism. It wasn't long before we began to hear reports about Jews who had survived the Holocaust being killed by Poles while attempting to regain their property. There was a murderous pogrom against returning Jews in Kielce, which sent a frightening message to all of the survivors. We should have better prospects for a new start in Germany.

We therefore decided that Yossel, Mother, and Laya would go back to Magdeburg, and find a place where we could all live together, while laying the groundwork for our new life. Our ultimate hope was to go to Israel or to the United States. Our departure from Nowa Ruda was given an unexpected boost when the

Russians decided that they needed the whole house, and gave us short notice to vacate.

We were very happy to be all living together in Magdeburg, but it soon became apparent that our sources of income were inadequate. We received some assistance from some Jewish relief groups, which was greatly appreciated, but it was just enough to pay for the bare necessities. In an effort to make some financial progress, we reluctantly agreed that the best plan would be to split up, with Issa, Moishe, and me going to the DP (Displaced Persons) camp at Fuerth, near Nuernberg, while Yossel, Mother, and Laya stayed in Magdeburg, and Father commuted between the two branches of the family.

Mother hadn't been really healthy for a long time, but it wasn't in her nature to complain about her own problems. Her concern was always for the rest of the family. Therefore, at the time of liberation, we were not fully aware of how sick she really was, but we couldn't help noticing that she was becoming very weak. She finally revealed to those who were living with her that she had been experiencing severe headaches for some time. Several visits to doctors in Magdeburg proved fruitless, and she was getting worse. People whom they knew and trusted told Father and Yossel that there were better doctors in Berlin, so they took Mother there, and left Laya to take care of the house in Magdeburg. Mother was taken immediately to a hospital in the American zone, but her condition continued to deteriorate. On July 8, 1945 our beloved mother passed away. The true heart of our family, whose indomitable spirit gave us strength when times were the bleakest, was lost forever. We find some comfort in knowing that her dream, that she should see her family safe and well after the war, had been fulfilled.

The only Jewish cemetery still available in Berlin was in the Russian zone; therefore, that was where our mother was laid to rest. Not realizing that Mother's condition was terminal, those of us living in Fuerth weren't told of her illness. Therefore, no letter was sent to us until she had died. When the letter arrived, I was alone in the house. I opened and read the letter, but my mind was not prepared to accept its message. I knew that my cousin Moishe Altman was very sick, so somehow my brain, unwilling to absorb the truth, made the substitution from my mother to my cousin, and I understood the letter to say that he had died. When Moishe came home, I handed him the letter, saying, "We got this letter from Yossel this morning. Cousin Moishe has died."

My brother read the letter, and then looked at me with open-mouthed disbelief.

"Why do you say Cousin Moishe died? This letter doesn't say that at all! It says that Mother died!"

I sat for some time in a state of shock, but finally got up the courage to read the letter again, and had to face the awful truth.

We knew that if we were to attend the funeral, we had to leave immediately, so we set off for Berlin as quickly as possible. Getting there required bypassing the Russian border guards by hiking over mountain passes, but despite our best efforts, we arrived too late for the funeral, mostly because the postal service had taken several days to deliver the letter.

None of us wanted to remain in Germany for an extended period of time, but such was to be the case. We were given the choice of being put on the list to go either to Israel or to the United States. We elected to go to the U. S., primarily because Father's brother Harry, who had emigrated before the war, was living in Los Angeles. The list was long and the quotas were small. During the waiting period two of my brothers got married. Yossel met a girl from Magdeburg named Lena Augenreich, and became the first to tie the knot. Then Issa married one of my girlfriends, Sally Rafawovich from Sosnowiec, who was a survivor, of the Majdanek death camp. Although we were still far down on the quota list, Uncle Harry was able to sponsor one person to come to Los Angeles. Moishe was selected, and thus became the first to emigrate to America. Five years after the end of the war, Father, Laya and I embarked on a former military transport ship and set sail from Bremerhaven bound for New York.

I was seasick from the time we left the harbor for the entire two week voyage, but my spirits couldn't have been higher as we stood with moistened eyes, leaning on the starboard railing, gliding past the Statue of Liberty. Alongside our fellow cargo of reborn souls, as we gazed at this beautiful symbol of Deliverance, we were filled with joy and hope, but our hearts could only rise so far, anchored by the dreadful memory from that distant shore, where the multitude of innocents were tortured and murdered in the most heinous way. The cry of those tortured souls will always echo in our hearts: "Never forget us!"

It took more than forty years for me to gather the courage to visit Bendzin again. I went with my sister Rae (Laya) and Rae's brother-in-law Alfred Harvey, another rare Bendzin survivor. What we found was a Polish town inhabited by living Polish people, but haunted by tens of thousands of Jewish spirits. I could feel their presence everywhere I turned. I wonder if those people who are living there today ever sense this other presence. These spirits are pleading to be remembered and the living are doing their best to ignore them.

Where are my neighbors, my girl friends, all my relatives outside my immediate family? I know where to find them.

If you travel to the gently rolling farmland of southwest Poland, near the small city of Oswiencim you will find a former pasture abutting a grove of aging birch trees. Within this field lie the remnants of the most efficient and most productive mass murder factory ever devised by Evil. This is *Birkenau*, named for those innocent birches at it border. The very mention of this name sends shudders down our spines—or it should. The raw materials for this factory were helpless men, women, children, and babies. The end product was foul smelling smoke and gray ashes. The production rate was often 10,000 lives extinguished per day.

Walking near the ruins of one of the four crematoria, we came to a small pond, perhaps 30 to 40 feet across. Frogs, crouching on the lily pads that floated on the water, basked in the gentle sunshine. The depression allowing for the rain to fill this pond is the result of the settling of ashes in a gigantic pit. As our little group stood by the pond to say Kaddish, I knelt down and picked up a small handful of the soil from the bank. The brown clay was mixed with hundreds of minute pieces of white bone ash. Staring at these tiny chips of charred bone, my mind shifted back to my carefree childhood and my little friend Rutka, who was born on the same day as I was, and who loved to run and play and giggle with me. Could these little white flecks in the mud be all that is left of her? I won't forget you, Rutka.

We waited a long time to come to America, but it was more than worth the waiting. Our family has accepted the opportunities that Freedom has offered us, and we have, all in all, had very rewarding lives in this wonderful country.

After arriving here, Moishe met and married an American girl, Sara Spielberg, whom we all called Sally. They were blessed with a daughter, Betsy, and two granddaughters. Sadly, we lost both Moishe and Sally in 2003. Although often questioned about it, Moishe never revealed the process for altering the ID papers. He carried this secret with him to the grave.

Laya, now Rae, married another survivor from Bendzin, Joseph Hamburger, who with his brother Alfred are the only survivors of their entire family. They were blessed with two fine sons, Phillip and Bruce, and five grandchildren. Shortly after being married they understandably changed their name to Harvey. Joe passed away in 2002.

Yossel and Lena had a daughter, Perla, while still in Germany, and now have two grandchildren.

Issa and Sally were married for over fifty years, until Issa's death in 2005. Although they had no children, they enjoyed a long, prosperous life together.

My father lived to be 102 years old. Before he passed away, he was honored in a special ceremony in Los Angeles for being the oldest living Holocaust survivor.

Zosza, my "older sister" in camp, survived the war, and we still see each other from time to time.

Sadly, in the chaos of our lives following liberation my dear Perka and I lost touch and I don't know what happened to her after we parted. She is in my prayers.

In spite of the Old World tradition of marrying off the daughters in order of birth, I was the last to marry. My husband, Louis Rabinowitz, was an American from Pennsylvania. Two years later tragedy struck: Louis was diagnosed with cancer, and died very shortly afterwards. My marriage with Louis rewarded me with the greatest treasure of my life—my son Allen. Being a widow with an infant and with very little education or training, life for me was very difficult for many years. In 1960 I met my current husband, Ralph Martin, and life has been very good to us.

Liberation brought us a new life; however, none of us were destined for a truly normal life. For the rest of our lives, we have all had difficulty in finding joy. I very seldom laugh. It is impossible to put the past behind, and to live for the future. Our children and grandchildren have been a marvelous source of pleasure, but the horrors of our early years are ever-present in our lives. The years of bombardment by constant fear inflicted deep wounds on our souls. The wounds may scar-over, but they are easily reopened and can never be completely healed. We are assaulted by frequent reminders of the past, and often wake up screaming from nightmares. This is, of course, the fate of most Holocaust survivors.

Ellie Wiesel, in *A Beggar in Jerusalem*, tells of a Jewish survivor in an insane asylum who believes that he is delusional because he knows that it is not possible that his beloved Jewish community could have totally disappeared from the face of the earth. The rest of us survivors can only envy this man—wouldn't it be far more merciful if we could believe that we are insane and that the Holocaust is only our delusion, rather than to know the truth?

In August 2000, Ralph and I founded the *Martin-Springer Institute* for *Applying the Lessons of the Holocaust, to Promote Altruism, Moral Courage and Tolerance,* at Northern Arizona University. In September, 2007 the *Center for Conflict Studies and Negotiation,* at Ben Gurion University of the Negev in Beersheba, Israel, pioneered by Professor Dan Baron, was renamed the *Martin-Springer Center for Conflict Studies and Negotiation.* Both of these institutions are dedicated in honor of the Springer family and the millions of victims of the Holocaust.

We pray that the work of these groups, and some miracles, such as those that saved our family, will be spread around the world, and humanity will someday learn that we are all members of one big family.

As a final note, I would like to put in the record that we are all aware that we could not have survived those perilous years without the clever planning, and a great many acts of daring, on the part of my brothers, Moishe and Yossel. We owe them an eternal debt of gratitude.

HOLOCAUST CHRONOLOGY
(Partially excerpted from: Holocaust Education
Foundation, Inc.) 1

*Note: Dates of Szpringer family
events are approximate.*

1933

January 30
President Hindenburg appoints Adolf Hitler as Reich Chancellor.

February 27
Reichstag burns; Decree issued overriding all guarantees of freedom.

March 22
Dachau concentration camp established.

April 1
Nazi proclaim a general boycott of all Jewish owned businesses.

April 7
Laws for Reestablishment of Civil Service barred Jews from holding civil service, university and state positions as well as being denied admission to the bar.

May 10
Public burning of books written by Jews, political dissidents, communists and other opponents of Nazism.

July 14
Law stripping East European Jewish immigrants of German citizenship.

September—Dora enters first grade.

October 3
Germany resigns from the League of Nations and the Geneva Disarmament Conference.

1934

January
Germany signs a nonaggression pact with Poland.

June27
Night of the Long Knives. Death of Ernst Rohm.

August 2
Death of Hindenburg. Hitler becomes Head of State and Commander in Chief of the Armed Forces.

1935
Szpringers move to new home and acquire a store.

Summer
Juden Verboten (No Jews) signs increase in numbers outside towns, villages, restaurants and stores.

September 15
Reichstag passes anti-Semitic "Nuremburg Laws." Jews no longer considered German citizens; could not marry Aryans or fly the German flag.

November 15
Germany defines a "Jew" as anyone with three Jewish grandparents or someone with two Jewish grandparents who identifies as a Jew.

1936

March 3
Jewish doctors barred from practicing medicine in German institutions.

March 7
Germany remilitarizes and occupies the Rhineland.

June 17
Himmler appointed the Chief of German Police.

September—Laya enters first grade

October 25
Hitler and Mussolini form Rome-Berlin Axis.

1937

July 16
Buchenwald Concentration Camp opens.

1938

March 13
Anschluss or union with Austria. A priority of Hitler to have Austria join with Germany Austrian government was bullied in to this union, though some Austrians wanted it.

April 26
Mandatory registration of all property held by Jews inside the Reich.

July 6
International conference at Evian, France fails to provide refuge for German Jews.

August
Adolph Eichmann establishes the Office of Jewish Emigration in Vienna to increase the pace of forced emigration.

September 29
Munich Conference: Great Britain and France agree to German occupation of the Sudetenland section of Czechoslovakia.

October 15
Germans mark all Jewish passports with a large letter "J."

November 7
Herschel Grynszpan, whose parents were deported from Germany to Poland, assassinates Ernest von Roth, Third Secretary of the German Embassy in Paris. This gives Germans an excuse for Kristallnacht.

November 9
Kristallnacht (Night of Broken Glass), anti-Semitic riots in Germany, Austria, and Sudetenland; 200 synagogues destroyed and 7,500 Jewish shops looted.

November 12
26,000 Jews are arrested and sent to concentration camps.

November 15
Jewish students are expelled from German schools.

December 12
One billion mark fine levied against German Jews for the destruction of property during Kristallnacht.

December 13
Decree on "Aryanization" is enacted. Compulsory expropriation of Jewish industries, businesses, and shops.

1939

January 30
Hitler in Reichstag speech, "If war erupts it will mean the Vernichtung (extermination) of European Jews."

July 26

Adolph Eichmann is placed in charge of the Prague branch of the Jewish Emigration Office.

August 23

Molotov - Ribbentrop Pact signed: nonaggression treaty between Germany and Soviet Union.

September 1

Germany invades Poland.

September 3

Great Britain and France declare war on Germany

September 4—The Wehrmacht conquers Bendzin.

September 9—Nazis burn the Synagogue and homes with people inside.
–Issa flees to Russia.

September 17

Soviet occupation of Eastern Poland.

September 21

Heydrich issues directives to establish ghettos in German-occupied Poland.

October 12

First deportation of Jews from Austria and Moravia to Poland.

October 28

First Polish ghetto established.

November—Theo Lalushna takes over the Szpringer's shoe store.

November 23
Wearing of Judenstern (yellow six pointed Star of David) is made compulsory throughout occupied Poland.

1940

April 9
Germany invades Denmark and Norway

April 30
Lodz Ghetto sealed: 165,000 people in 1.6 square miles.

May 10
Germany invades Holland, Belgium, and France.

May 22
Auschwitz concentration camp established.

June 22
France surrenders to Germany

September 27
Berlin-Rome-Tokyo Axis is established.

November 15
Warsaw Ghetto sealed: contains 500,000 people.

1941

January 21-26
Anti-Jewish riots in Romania

March 17
Adolph Eichmann appointed head of the department for Jewish affairs of the Reich Main Security Office, Section II B4.

June 22
Germany invades the Soviet Union.

July 8
Wearing the Jewish star in the German occupied Baltic States is required.

July 31
Heydrich is appointed by Goring to carry out the "Final Solution" (extermination of all Jews in Europe).

September 15
Wearing of the Jewish star is decreed throughout the Greater Reich.

September 23
First experiments with gassing are made at Auschwitz.

September 28/29
35,000 Jews are massacred at Babi Yar outside Kiev.

October 8
Establishment of Auschwitz II (Birkenau) for extermination of Jews, Gypsies, and Slavic people.

October 10
Theresienstadt Ghetto in Czechoslovakia is established.

October 14
Deportation of German Jews begins.

October 23
Massacre in Odessa: 34,000 killed.

October 24
Massacre in Kiev: 34,000 killed.

November 6
Massacre in Rovno: 15,000 killed.

December 7
Japanese attack Pearl Harbor.

December 8
U.S. declares war on Japan. Chelmno extermination camp on the Ner River in Poland is opened. Massacre in Riga: 27,000 killed.

December 11
Germany declares war on U.S.

December 22
Massacre in Vilna: 32,000 killed.

1942

January 20
Wannsee Conference on Nazi "Final Solution of the Jewish Question." Heydrich outlines plan to murder Europe's Jews.

March 17
Extermination program begins in Belzec; by the end of 1942, 600,000 Jews will have been murdered.

June 1
Treblinka Extermination camp opens. Wearing of Jewish star is decreed in Nazi occupied France and Holland.

July 22
300,000 Jews from the Warsaw Ghetto are deported to Treblinka.

July 28
Jewish resistance organization is established in the Warsaw Ghetto.

August 12—Szpringer family survives intact from the selection in the sport stadium.

October 17
Allied nations pledge to punish Germany for the policy of genocide.

Autumn—Dora sent to concentration camp.

1943

January—Josef Jarosz takes over the Szpringer shoe store.
     The Szpringers are forced to move to the ghetto in the Kamionka.

January 18
Jews in Warsaw Ghetto launch uprising against Nazi deportations. Fighting lasts four days.

February 2
German Sixth Army surrenders at Stalingrad. This marks the war's turning point.

March—Moishe is fired from the shoe store by Jarosz.

April 19
Warsaw Ghetto revolt begins as Germans attempt to liquidate 70,000 inhabitants.

May 16
Warsaw Ghetto liquidated.

June 11
Himmler orders liquidation of all Polish ghettos.

August 1–Judenrein begins in Bendzin.

August 2
Revolt at Treblinka death camp.

August 16
Revolt in Bialystok Ghetto.

September—The Szpringers go to Jelesnia.

September 23
Vilna Ghetto liquidated.

October 14
Armed revolt in Sobibor Extermination camp.

November—Father (Jan) and Moishe (Mietek) go to Moeckern.

1944
March—Laya (Poilka), Yossel (Jusek) and Mother (Bronslowa) arrive in Magdeburg.

March 19
Germany occupies Hungary.

May 15
Nazis begin deporting Hungarian Jews. By June 27, 380,000 sent to Auschwitz.

June 6
D-Day Normandy Invasion: Allies begin liberation of Western Europe.

July 20
Group of German officers attempt to assassinate Hitler.

July 24
Soviet troops liberate Majdanek extermination camp.

November 7
Revolt at Auschwitz; one crematorium is destroyed.

November 8
40,000 Jews forced to participate in the Budapest to Austria death march.

November 24
Himmler orders destruction of Auschwitz crematorium to hide evidence of Nazi death camps.

1945

January 17
Soviet troops liberate Warsaw. Auschwitz evacuated; inmate death march begins.

January 25
Stutthof concentration camp evacuated; death march of inmates begins.

April 15
British troops liberate Bergen-Belsen death camp.

April 25
American and Soviet troops meet at the Elbe River.

April 30
Hitler commits suicide.

May 7
V-E Day Germany surrenders unconditionally.

July—Mother passes away.

August 15
Japan surrenders unconditionally

November 22
Nuremburg War Crimes Tribunal commences.

1946

October 1
Nuremburg Trials conclude with a judgment in which twelve defendants were sentenced to death, three to life imprisonment, four to various prison terms, and three acquitted.